ALAIN BUFFARD

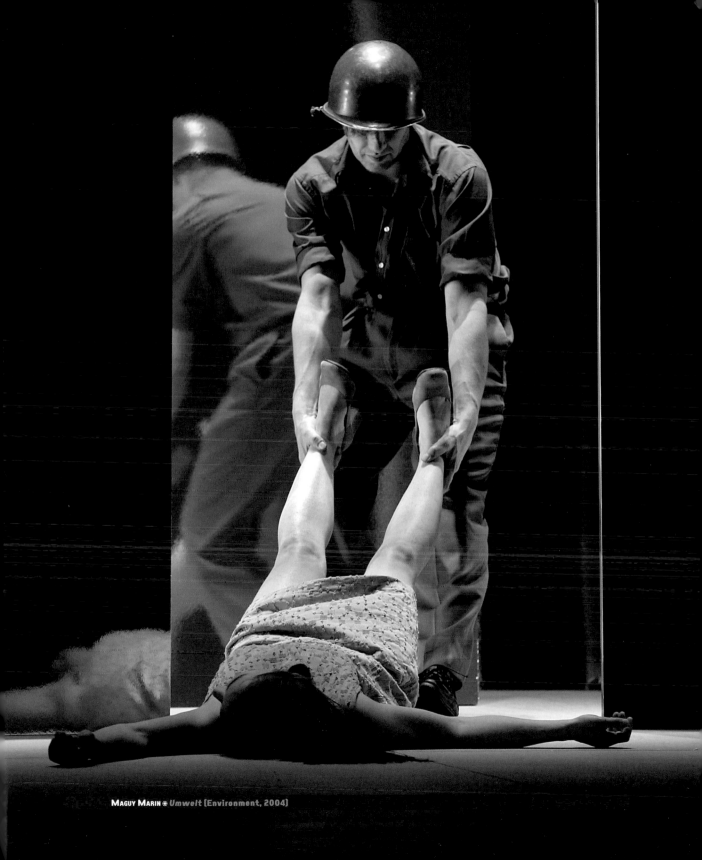

MAGUY MARIN ⊛ *Umwelt* (Environment, 2004)

MEMBROS ✦ *Febre* (Fever, 2007)

SANKAI JUKU ⊛ *Utsuri* (Virtual Garden, 2003)

ANNE TERESA DE KEERSMAEKER ⊗ *D'un soir un jour* (A Day in a Night, 2006)

SERIES EDITED BY ÉLISABETH COUTURIER

PHILIPPE NOISETTE

talk about contemporary dance

Flammarion

CONTENTS

1 DID YOU SAY CONTEMPORARY DANCE? *page 13*

2 WHAT'S THE POINT OF DANCE TODAY? *page 33*

3 DANCE MYTHS *page 51*

4 IF YOU LIKE... *page 77*

5 KEY WORDS *page 137*

6 KEY DATES *page 141*

7 THEY DARED TO DO IT *page 161*

8 RISQUÉ PARTNERS *page 169*

9 30 DANCERS/CHOREOGRAPHERS *page 187*

APPENDIXES *page 249*

PREFACE

When I moved to Paris some thirty years ago to complete my education, I quickly acquired a taste for outings to the theater. One evening, at a venue called Les Gémeaux in Sceaux, just outside Paris, something clicked. It was in the mid-1980s, when a wonderful new wave of young choreographers was breaking over France. *Codex*, the somewhat mysterious name of the show that evening, suddenly opened my eyes: so *that's* what dance could be—a riot of props, colors, sounds, and sensations, with bodies of every shape and size. There was laughter and wonder, creating an entirely new dimension. Philippe Decouflé, the choreographer, had earned some recognition in high-profile dance companies led by Alwin Nikolais and Régine Chopinot, then quickly struck out on his own in the early 1980s. He was still an up-and-coming young man, not yet the media star who staged the 1992 Winter Olympic Games in Albertville and other glamorous events.

When the show ended that evening, my date and I went to see Decouflé to ask if I could make an appointment to interview him. As one thing led to another, contemporary dance became my overriding passion—and then my profession. Until then I had been unsure what I wanted to write about, but since that time I have never stopped living and breathing dance. Obviously, I ventured back in time in order to learn where these choreographers and performers were coming from, and my path inevitably crossed the likes of Sergey Diaghilev and his Ballets Russes, Isadora Duncan, Maurice Béjart, and many other figures. I also accompanied the careers of a number of newcomers: Alain Platel, a spirited Fleming whom I discovered by chance at the one and only occurrence of a "dance biennial" at a Belgian university, the marvelous Maguy Marin, who has embodied a socially committed yet always poetic art, from *May B* to *Umwelt* via *Cinderella* and *Turba*; William Forsythe, of course, who had been performing regularly in Paris for years and who had the elegance to willingly discuss philosophy or politics with me after his opening nights; Pina Bausch, who agreed to a meeting in "her" cluttered dance studio (a converted movie theater); and even Merce Cunningham, from whom I stole a few moments following one rehearsal, and who invited me to watch one of his favorite female dancers. I now miss Pina and Merce, as no doubt many readers do. But then there is always Jérôme Bel, conceptual dance's "agent provocateur," who with a few well-considered works has set creative choreography back on the path of intelligent polemic; as indicated in the title of one of his innovating pieces: *The Show Must Go On*.

That's what I really like about the dance scene—by the time one trend wanes, two or three new ones are already elbowing their way in. Looking back in history, I discovered the substantial wealth of an art often considered minor simply because it is ephemeral. Long before dance became "contemporary," pioneers had explored, experimented, failed—and succeeded. Many upheavals originated in America, where Martha Graham rejected the classical path and opened the way for peerless dancers such as Merce Cunningham. In Japan, the masters of Butoh looked back upon a strong tradition the better to recast it. In Europe, German Expressionist dance produced many offshoots including the formal explorations of French modern dancers Françoise and Dominique Dupuy. Wherever I look on the map of dance, I see landmarks and beckoning signs. The landscape is constantly shifting and expanding, now ranging from Africa to Asia.

The real point of this book probably lies in one basic observation: dance, being based on the human body, is a universal art, yet one that more than ever needs to reach out to its audience. This volume cannot cover everything, but it is designed to point readers in the right directions. It even glances back a century or two, just as it projects a dialogue between present and future. I wrote it with readers in mind, from the first page to the last. Reader, I'm sure we share the same love of movement—and we never know where a dance performance may lead us.

PHILIPPE NOISETTE

ALAIN PLATEL ✳ *Pitié* (Pity, 2008)

DID YOU SAY CONTEMPORARY DANCE?

HOW CAN YOU RECOGNIZE IT?

One of the revolutions attributed to contemporary dance arises from the many forms it takes on stage. Everything—or almost—is permitted when it comes to length of performance, costumes, and sets. Everything seems to be invented— or reinvented—in real time.

Angelin Preljocaj, *Les 4 Saisons…* (The Four Seasons, 2005), Sergio Diaz and Kaori Ito. A fruitful collaboration with artist Fabrice Hyber produced crazy, wonderful costumes and sets.

Dancers tread the stage barefoot, or in shoes, or high heels, or platform boots or even, occasionally, in ballet slippers. When it comes to costume, anything goes: after the tutu, leotard, and tights came a period of jeans, undergarments, overalls, business suits, evening (or wedding) gowns, sweat suits, designer outfits, day-glo jumpsuits— and nudity.

It's all a question of body. Gone are the days of uniformity, and even though certain contemporary choreographers reflexively choose the same physical type of dancer, performances can be executed by the large and small, the fat and thin, black and white, Africans and Asians, very young and very old, stars and unknowns, professionals and beginners.

Since contemporary dance knows no boundaries, and since the corps de ballet has withered away, everything is possible, from a minimalist solo to a choral dance for a hundred. Duets and trios abound, sometimes due to lack of resources, whereas some leading choreographers boast dance companies of twenty or more members. Nor it is forbidden to summon on stage a bunch of amateurs, an orchestra, animals of all kinds, little children, a local marching band, an actor, a pianist, athletes, or even the choreographer's mother (and father).

As we shall see, it is also a question of gender: male-female, female-female, male-male, and all hybrids in between. Some wear wigs, others prosthetic devices, and some even flaunt, depending on mood, total emotional confusion. Who says that (contemporary) dance isn't sexy?

Once the cast has been chosen, the audience will still be confronted with an endless variety of sets and stagings: a field of carnations, a green lawn, a pond, a rock, sails, canvases, tarpaulins, a merry-go-round, a shopping mall, a dance floor, a ritzy living room, a derelict housing project, a forest, a peat marsh, an inflatable structure, a boxing ring, a podium, a row of spotlights with the fog of smoke machines, a clutch of chairs with a bunch of tables, silvery objects labeled Andy Warhol, photographs by Robert Rauschenberg, bugs in the manner of Fabrice Hyber, clay contributed by Miquel Barceló, and branches gathered by Andy Goldsworthy.

All that remains to be done is to bring dance to life in these more or less cluttered landscapes. Some choreographers opt for minimalism, indeed motionlessness, while others prefer physical energy. Some favor diagonal dynamics, others fervently defend floor work. Crazy DJ choreographers combine hip-hop moves with contemporary and African dance, and acrobats fly through the air. Then there are the sporty types, and even purists who swear by a pas de deux (which, if things click, can also evolve into a trio—or more).

Note, however, that contemporary dance is not synonymous with chaos. Thanks to their training—and almost every one has had some—choreographers manage to create harmony from apparent disorder. Sometimes nothing is more ordered than a performance of contemporary dance, even those pieces designed to shatter conventions.

In order to escape constraints that were once mandatory, contemporary dance often exits the theater as soon as it can. The boldest choreographers "do" dance on the roof of a skyscraper or the runway of an airport, in a football field or an indoor pool, an abandoned factory or a trendy gallery, a green meadow or a coal mine, a museum or the façade of some building, a riverside quay or a public park, a skating rink or a circus ring. For that matter, who knows whether right this minute someone isn't devising a pas de deux on the moon—complete with spacesuit and weightlessness—or a performance in the depths of the sea? The main thing is not to know whether something *is* possible but to *believe* that it is—at least a little. After all, to quote Jean Cocteau's quip to Sergey Diaghilev, there is no better motto for contemporary dance than, "Amaze me!"

RIGHT
Alain Platel,
vsprs (2006).
Monteverdi's *Vespers*
set in a mountain
of underwear.

FOLLOWING PAGES
Alain Platel,
Wolf (2004).
An urban ballet with
dancers and opera
singers, skillfully
directed and set in an
ersatz shopping mall.

HOW CAN YOU DEFINE IT?

The very expression "contemporary dance," used for the past forty years or so, still bothers some people even though we are now well into the third artistic millennium. Why? Perhaps because the term is too vague, too austere, or carries too many connotations. So it is important to state (and write) that contemporary dance can be serious, funny, bold, ironic, brutal, factual, daring, artistic, or urban. It is precisely this range of tastes that provides the spice.

Unlike other fields of art, the still-young realm of contemporary dance does not hesitate to call itself into question, to explore unknown territory, and to cozy up to the worlds of music, art, imagery, and fashion. It thereby remains terribly up-to-date, as though constantly connected to a source of ongoing stimulation. Its language seems to undergo perpetual mutation—after a performance of contemporary dance you often hear people in the audience exclaim, "It's amazing what the body can do!" Which is a good sign.

In almost every country with a history of ballet (whether venerable, as in France and Russia, or more recent, as in the United States), choreographers strive to reconceptualize both the form and content of dance.

The origin of this state of mind can be associated, although not exclusively, with the idea of "radical break." When a performing artist such as the American Merce Cunningham played with chance, employed video technology, or taught himself computer-aided choreographic composition at various points in a long artistic career that began in the 1950s, he created a rupture with the narrative dance that he himself had previously studied and performed. Audiences initially rejected his efforts, apart from a small group of loyal admirers who always considered him to be a pioneering master well ahead of his time, right up to his death in the summer of 2009. Ironically, some young choreographers now view Cunningham as a classicist. Meanwhile, advocates of post-modern dance in the 1960s (a group of choreographers who rejected the virtuosity of both classical ballet and modern dance*) stressed their distance from Cunningham as a founding father. Two decades later, Pina Bausch in Germany triggered a similar kind of break when she became director of the Wuppertal Opera Ballet, a rather isolated neo-classical troupe; after a few initial pieces that were still legible to Wuppertal audiences, the rupture widened as Bausch developed her idea of Tanztheater (dance-theater, which is more than a mere blend of dance and dramatic events), in which dancers even spoke lines between their moves! The death of Bausch in June 2009, followed a few days later by that of Cunningham, seemed to bring a somewhat belated end to a twentieth century rich in choreographic invention. It is still too early to wager on the radical breaks that will mark—or not—the new millennium, but the foundations laid by these two pioneers are solid, and their works should stand the test of time.

FACING PAGE (TOP LEFT)
Régine Chopinot,
K.O.K. (1988).
A ring and phony boxers in oversized shorts by Jean-Paul Gaultier: *K.O.K.* is an irreverent tribute to the world of boxing with its furiously dance-like moves.

FACING PAGE (TOP RIGHT)
Jean-Claude Gallotta,
Ulysse (*Ulysses*, 1981, revived 1993).
This ballet in white, about leave-takings, is typical of Gallotta's style: body-to-body duets, careering dancers, and sundry tricks.

FACING PAGE (BOTTOM LEFT)
Maguy Marin,
May B. (1981).
Inspired by the writings of Samuel Beckett, *May B.* featured world-weary individuals dressed in shapeless costumes, their bodies smeared in white. Its impact was so great that it is still performed around the world, thirty years later.

FACING PAGE (BOTTOM RIGHT)
Pina Bausch,
Kontakthof (1978).
German choreographer Pina Bausch spearheaded the Tanztheater (dance theater) movement, which often dealt with intense male-female relationships.

* See key words, p. 137–39

In France in the late 1970s young choreographers "declared war" on a mandatory style of modern dance forged by visionaries such as Maurice Béjart and appreciated by a wide audience. Yet Béjart himself had made a break with classical and neoclassical ballet by dressing his dancers in jeans, using Indian music, and performing in venues previously used only for rock concerts.

ABOVE

Merce Cunningham, *Scenario* (1997), Merce Cunningham Dance Company. Dance without a story line, but with great impact. Here designer Rei Kawakubo's costumes, with artificial bulges, contrast with Cunningham's pure

FACING PAGE

Jean-Claude Gallotta, *Cher Ulysse* (Dear Ulysses, revived 2007). Gallotta revived a key work from the 1980s with a different company, rewriting his own history of dance.

The French new wave was ready to use everything, including the kitchen sink: Jean-Claude Gallotta combined professionals with amateurs who had no serious dance training; Maguy Marin effaced gender in the way she made-up men and women; Régine Chopinot hung dancers on ropes that sent their steps flying. This movement put an end to slick performances and the mere telling of tales. A new torch was held aloft by contemporary dance, whether abstract or dramatic—or expressive. But contemporary dance also developed—or imposed—its own rules, perhaps in reaction to the chaos that followed the sociopolitical upheavals of May 1968. Whatever the case, thanks to its liberation of the body and its new vision of the world, contemporary dance invented its own history. Which it continues to write.

WHEN AND WHERE DID IT BEGIN?

Until the day a scientist isolates the DNA for dance—especially its contemporary species—we will just have to settle for a few key dates that mark the evolution of twentieth-century choreography. Indeed, it was during this amazing century that dance would undergo successive cultural revolutions spanning several continents.

Merce Cunningham, *Split Sides* (2003), Merce Cunningham Dance Company.
As the human link between modern and postmodern dance in America, Cunningham constantly innovated by multiplying points of view.

The vocabulary of dance is sometimes misleading. For example, in the United States, that hothouse of creativity, people tend to refer to "modern dance" (early twentieth century) and "postmodern dance" (from the 1960s onward). Yet to a certain extent they lack a term for what came in between, namely the advent of a figure such as Merce Cunningham, who revolutionized the approach to dance worldwide. In fact, Cunningham was a pivotal figure in this transition: from 1939 to 1945 he was a dancer in the company led by Martha Graham, a pioneer of modern dance who sought to cut the tie to academic ballet; by 1944 Cunningham was choreographing his own solos; in the following years, he brought together musicians and artists associated with the experimental community at Black Mountain College in North Carolina. In 1953 Cunningham founded his own company. Many of the performers who passed through his studio at one time or another would subsequently forge the trend known as postmodern dance, which was opposed both to modern dance and to the Cunningham technique, which they felt was not radical enough. So does that make Cunningham a modern choreographer or a postmodern choreographer? In fact, he was—and always will be—just Cunningham, a visionary.

America can thus lay claim to contemporary dance. Even when the wind blows in the other direction, or drops completely, the American flag still flies over the modern spirit.

In Europe, there was a time lag between Germany and France. In Germany, a number of choreographers invented, or attempted to invent, a type of dance that broke with the classical past. The 1930s were marked by Kurt Jooss (choreographer and teacher) and Mary Wigman (dancer and choreographer). The rise of Nazism put an end to many careers, yet Germany remained in the forefront. In the 1950s and 1960s, a renaissance hinted at the emergence of a truly contemporary dance.

PAGE 24
Françoise and Dominique Dupuy, *L'Estran* (Foreshore, 2005). Wu Zheng and Françoise Dupuy: the torch is passed from one generation to the next.

PAGE 25
Anna Halprin, *Parades and Changes* (1965–67), here *Parades and Changes Replay* (2008). Initially censored in the United States, this scandalous ballet celebrated nudity in all its glory.

Pina Bausch, *Nelken* (Carnations, 1982). Half-acted, half-danced scenes take place on a carpet of carnations.

In France, the 1950s were marked by the arrival of figures such as Karin Waehner from Germany and Jerome Andrews from America. Such artists were often former pupils of Wigman. But attempts to forge a specifically French modern dance—a sibling to its American elder—were awkward. One of the first, nearly "contemporary," accomplishments was the founding of the Ballet Théâtre Contemporain (1968–78). This company of roughly forty dancers was designed to perform pieces by contemporary choreographers, both French and foreign. So were the 1970s "contemporary" in France? Initiatives in all direction claimed to be contemporary in intent, for example the Théâtre du Silence headed by Jacques Garnier and Brigitte Lefèvre (who twenty-five years later would be appointed director of the Paris Opera Ballet) and the Félix Blaska Company. Usually these initiatives were taken by former classical dancers. Two American dancers made their mark in France during this decade, namely Carolyn Carlson (first with the Paris Opera Ballet, where she headed a quasi-autonomous unit, and later as a solo dancer) and Susan Buirge. **So when added to the effect of Cunningham, Alwin Nikolais, and, later, Trisha Brown, American influence had a dominant impact on future French trends. But it was not the only influence, because Tanztheater and Butoh also had their followers. "New," hence contemporary, dance in France was largely a post-1968 accomplishment. From the dance competition launched in Bagnolet to the establishment of national dance centers, the story of contemporary dance in France finally got off the ground.**

WHAT WERE ITS ROOTS?

Freeing themselves from the yoke of classical ballet that rose to the fore in the nineteenth century, choreographers in the early twentieth century sought to invent a new, as yet nameless, form of dance. They rechanneled, rather than rejected, the heritage of ballet, dragging audiences along in a great hullabaloo that might well have pleased Terpsichore, muse of music and dance. This (re)birth of dance gave rise to a spirited, prodigal generation of contemporary choreographers. However, on the old continent the new century was not only one of artistic revolution, but also of bloody warfare.

In Russia, a man whose artistic sensibility was matched by a good nose for business—and scandal—chose Paris as his launching pad. Sergey Diaghilev was both impresario and visionary. His innovative troupe, Les Ballets Russes, brought together dancers, choreographers, musicians, and artists. Instead of contenting himself with performances of *Giselle*, he placed his faith in choreographers such as Michel Fokine, Léonide Massine, and Serge Lifar. In a way, Diaghilev invented the modern dance troupe, the ancestor of today's dance companies.

What he did not foresee—or foresaw only too well—was the upheaval that a total artist such as Vaslav Nijinsky would unleash with landmark choreography for *The Rites of Spring* and *L'Après-midi d'un faune*. No tutus or arabesques here: instead, toes were turned inward, poses were borrowed from Greek statuary, and scores were commissioned from the likes of Igor Stravinsky and Claude Debussy. The chosen subjects of Russian folklore, sacrifice, and eroticism were a far cry from classical fairy tales. During the short lifespan of Diaghilev's company, collaborators included painters and poets of the stature of Picasso, Cocteau, Matisse, and Max Ernst.

In the wake of Les Ballets Russes, a Swedish art collector in Paris, Rolf de Maré, also boldly merged various genres, classically trained performers, and artists of all kinds in a dance company called Les Ballets Suédois. Its contribution has recently been fully acknowledged.

Vaslav Nijinsky, *L'Après-midi d'un faune* (Afternoon of a Faun, 1912). The unbridled sexuality of Nijinsky's faun made headlines when it was first performed at the Théâtre du Châtelet in Paris.

Bronislava Nijinska, *Les Noces* (The Wedding, 1923), here in a revival by the Ballet National de Lorraine (2008).
Inspired by Russian folklore, Stravinsky's score for *Les Noces* was choreographed for Les Ballets Russes by Nijinsky's sister, Bronislava Nijinska.

In Germany, the period was marked by the ideas of two men. Émile Jacques-Dalcroze, of Swiss origin, opened a dance institute in Hellerau in 1911 with the backing of a German patron. His method stressed the development of an inner ear (that is to say, a sense of musicality rather than virtuosity alone); his pupils would play a key role in the emergence of modern—if not yet contemporary—dance. **Choreographer and theorist Rudolf Laban was the other crucial figure who influenced future dancers and creative artists.** A utopian who devised improvisations and musical accompaniments inspired by nature (constituting an innovation at the time), Laban founded a system still taught today at the Laban Center in London.

An Expressionist trend subsequently grew around Mary Wigman, who was close to Laban and whose "students" included Dore Hoyer and, later, Susanne Linke. Advocating dance as a form of personal expression, Wigman imparted a certain independence to moves and steps, notably in terms of music—she even choreographed pieces to be performed in silence. Her tours of the United States from 1930 onward made a big impression. Meanwhile, other new links were being forged. Karin Waehner, who had worked with Wigman in Leipzig, moved to France in 1953, where she would teach as well as dance; later, her young pupils included the likes of Angelin Preljocaj. In Paris another German influenced by the expressionist trend, Jean Weidt, would encounter Françoise and Dominique Dupuy—partners in life as well as on stage—who were veritable forerunners of contemporary dance in France.

These various cross-fertilizations would culminate in the emergence of the contemporary dance movement in the late 1970s.

Another student of Laban, Kurt Jooss, choreographed pieces with political and social themes from the 1920s and 1930s onward, the most famous being *The Green Table*, a harbinger of the growing dread of a second world war. This work still figures in the repertoire of major dance companies. He also founded the Ballets Jooss, and revitalized dance at the Folkwang school following a period of exile in England during the Nazi regime. Jooss's "disciples" became the new wave of contemporary dancers that included Pina Bausch, the most influential German choreographer, whose Tanztheater took the world by storm in the 1970s.

In England, it was Marie Rambert, a ballerina originally in Diaghilev's Ballets Russes who catalyzed things. She founded a dance company rooted in classicism yet open to a certain modernity from the 1920s through the 1960s. In the 1980s the Rambert Dance Company took another step forward by inviting guest choreographers from broader horizons and by adopting the Cunningham technique.

FACING PAGE

Sankai Juku, *Utsuri* (Virtual Garden, 2003). Ushio Amagatsu retained Butoh's spare costumes and static pauses, but replaced the grotesque aspect with a ceremonial aesthetics.

ABOVE

Merce Cunningham, *Biped* (1999), Holley Farmer and Lisa Boudreau. Detectors on the dancers' bodies sent data to a computer, which projected the information onto the stage.

In France, the roots of dance are deep and often marked by a classical approach. In 1960 Maurice Béjart founded his own company, the Ballet of the 20th Century, not in France but in Brussels, Belgium, where he developed an increasingly theatrical style open to neoclassical, jazz, and even African dance. Above all, Béjart's school served as the crucible for a talented generation, ranging from Maguy Marin to Anne Teresa de Keersmaeker, that would soon head in its own direction. A branch of Béjart's school also opened, with some difficulty, in Senegal. The teaching offered in his schools—theater, music, and mime as well as dance—permanently broke down barriers in the dance movement. Contemporary dance—and dancers—owe Béjart a great deal, even if they do not always acknowledge it.

In the United States, rebellion paid off. Isadora Duncan quickly developed her own style, based on elegiac movement, a sense of liberation, and a recognition of femininity. Yet it was in Europe, where she moved in 1900, that Duncan received true recognition. Other choreographers, often women, sought inspiration from realms removed from Romantic, hence academic, ballet. Ruth St. Denis produced dance pieces influenced by Egypt, and later founded a dance school with her husband, Ted Shawn, which was attended by the cream of the future "modern dance" generation from Doris Humphrey to Charles Weidman, not forgetting Martha Graham, the movement's high priestess with her own distinctive style. The Graham technique involved contraction and release designed to free the body's energy. Graham's contribution, though still based on narratives that recounted Greek tragedies or American myths, was considerable. Through her teaching in particular she would influence an entire new movement of local choreographers. Merce Cunningham, probably the most exemplary figure of contemporary dance in America, was a member of Graham's company before he decided to take to his own wings like the *Birds* of the title of one of his works.

Meanwhile, Japan, a land of theatrical traditions that might appear somewhat rigid—Bunraku, Kabuki, and Noh—underwent an artistic upheaval that remained underground yet had clear repercussions. In 1959, following the tragedy of Hiroshima, Tatsumi Hijikata invented a form of dance called Butoh. This "dance of darkness" evolved into a neo-Butoh form that became popular in France and the United States, where some of Hijikata's disciples lived. In the 1970s, a Japanese rebel named Hideyuki Yano sought to establish a bridge between East and West in Paris; an early victim of AIDS, however, Yano did not live to witness the outcome, a dynamic link between past and present.

PAGE 30
Martha Graham, *Lamentation* (1930), here performed by the Ballet National de Lorraine in 2005. Making a break with classical ballet, the pioneering modern choreographer Martha Graham magnified the role of women on stage.

PAGE 31
Maurice Béjart, *Symphonie pour un homme seul* (Symphony for a Lone Man, 1955). The expressive, prodigal role of the dancer (Gil Roman) invites the audience to commune with dance.

FRÉDÉRIC FLAMAND, BALLET NATIONAL DE MARSEILLE ✳ *Métapolis* (2000)

WHAT'S THE POINT OF DANCE TODAY?

2

WHAT'S THE POINT OF DANCE TODAY?

IT'S DIFFERENT THAN BALLET

Fairy tales have turned sour, ballerinas have put away their toe shoes, and princes have sex (the act, not just the gender). Contemporary dance has rid the most body-oriented performing art of its somewhat old-fashioned image. Whereas a budding ballerina is less glamorous than a top model, hip-hop dancers have become highly popular figures.

ABOVE

Lucinda Childs, *Dance* (1979). Twin effect: live dancers on stage plus the projection of a film of Childs's ballet.

FACING PAGE (TOP)

Maurice Béjart, *Boléro* (1961). Nicolas Le Riche, star dancer with the Paris Opera Ballet, performs Béjart's vision of Maurice Ravel's score.

FACING PAGE (BOTTOM)

Maguy Marin, Lyon Opera Ballet, *Coppélia* (1993). Following the success of *Cinderella* with the same company, Marin attacked the classical legend of Coppelia, presented here as a blonde bombshell who swaps her toe shoes for high heels.

Anyone growing up in the postwar years who showed an interest in dance would inevitably have to deal with classical arabesques, a pas de deux in leotard (with optional tiara), and tales of ghosts in Romantic compositions. The arrival on the scene of a "total artist" like Maurice Béjart completely altered the situation. Already in rebellion against the classical institution, Béjart's choreography, from *Symphonie pour un homme seul* (Symphony for a Lone Man, 1955) to *Boléro* (1961) entailed new forms of theater and music (in collaboration with composers such as Pierre Boulez and Pierre Henry). Béjart appeared on television, used an indoors sports stadium as a dance venue, and even made a cameo appearance in the movies (Claude Lelouch's *Boléro*). Yet some people might object that Béjart was still not "contemporary"; perhaps not, but he was "almost modern." And he had come a long way from the hegemony of classical ballet, which threatened to wither to increasingly small groups of ballet lovers once the superstars had moved on to something else (such as Patrick Dupont and Sylvie Guillem in France, and Rudolf Nureyev, Margot Fonteyn, and Mikhail Baryshnikov elsewhere in Europe and the United States). Although the dominant impression is that contemporary dance attacked established norms, and hence classical ballet, it would be short-sighted to overlook the fact that new, creative blood infused all forms of dance, to everyone's great benefit. Thus a respectable establishment like the Paris Opera Ballet soon realized the advantage to be gained from a more contemporary approach to its repertoire. It was helped in this move by strong figures such as Nureyev (director from 1983 to 1989) and Brigitte Lefèvre; it also set up various experimental units and creative groups, namely the Groupe de Recherches Théâtrales de l'Opéra (Opera Theatrical Research Group, 1975, led by star dancer and choreographer Carolyn Carlson), followed by the Groupe de Recherche Chorégraphique (Choreographic Research Group). This latter unit, headed by Jacques Garnier, numbered roughly a dozen house dancers who explored contemporary techniques from 1981 to 1989—names such as Merce Cunningham and Paul Taylor began appearing on Opera posters, along with those choreographers'

postmodern offspring (Karole Armitage, Lucinda Childs) and a number of mavericks (Philippe Decouflé, Maguy Marin, and François Verret). The intentions were good—to present audiences with new works. Although there was a certain amount of incomprehension, some reputations were made. The Paris Opera Ballet company continued to feature its classics every season, sometimes in revamped versions (from *Swan Lake* to *La Bayadère* and *Sylvie* to *The Nutcracker*), which was its main raison-d'être, but also creations more in tune with contemporary choreography (by William Forsythe, Wayne McGregor, Angelin Preljocaj, Pina Bausch, Susanne Linke, Mats Ek). Resistance can still run high, however, as demonstrated by hostile audience reactions to the premiere at the historic opera house of *Véronique Doisneau* by Jérôme Bel, a leading figure in the realm of conceptual dance in the early 2000s.

FACING PAGE

Matthew Bourne, *Swan Lake* (1995). This musical-like version of *Swan Lake* sets the action in a very British royal family, where the prince falls in love with a male swan. A runaway hit.

ABOVE

Karole Armitage, Ballet National de Lorraine, *Rave* (2001). The classically trained Armitage pirated the vocabulary of ballet to forge an idiom inspired by the poses of models for *Vogue* magazine.

RIGHT

Jérôme Bel, *Véronique Doisneau* (2004). Commissioned by the Paris Opera Ballet, this portrait of a ballerina on the eve of retirement alternates personal story with danced illustration.

Not everything from classical ballet is to be thrown out. Far from it. An intelligent understanding of the mechanisms at work in the construction of Romantic and dramatic ballets can reinvigorate the classical idiom, as shown by crossover choreographers such as Mats Ek, William Forsythe, Matthew Bourne, and Maguy Marin. Ek's Giselle ends up in an asylum, Marin's Coppelia lives in a ghetto, Forsythe's star dancers sway their hips dangerously, and Bourne's prince from *Swan Lake* celebrates his coming-out in leather, flanked by male swans. The cultural revolution has thus clearly reached classical ballet, too.

IT REFLECTS OUR TIMES

A long time has passed since King Louis XIV of France learned ballet steps and enjoyed comedy-ballets studded with delightful deities and other theatrical machinery. Somewhat closer to our own times, Romantic ballet, with its courtly loves, flitting sprites, and other magical figures all vying for attention, has also lost its luster. Even though such dream worlds are not totally outlawed today, contemporary dance has turned to more modern concerns in an effort to understand other realms. Even better, it has done so without the need to teach people much more than a thing or two.

One of the standard complaints about classical ballet was precisely its fantasy world with characters from the past and codes completely removed from everyday life. True enough: whereas painting and theater have always tried to keep up with their times, ballet—notably Romantic ballet—remained stuck in an unfortunately "timeless" ideal.

Little by little, reality began to intervene as some choreographers drew inspiration from their personal lives and backgrounds. The emergence of contemporary dance also favored an elegant encounter between various schools of art. Abstraction quickly won points by refraining from any comment on current events. Yet the postmodern trend in the United States sought a more political stance. People were against the war in Vietnam, and for greater sexual liberation. In the late 1960s Yvonne Rainer presented works with explicit titles such as *M-Walk* and *War*. Dancer and choreographer Bill T. Jones, on the other hand, recounted not only his own illness from AIDS but also the condition of African-Americans in a land which at that time—the 1990s—could hardly dream of ever seeing a black man elected president. Jones's *Still Here* (1994) provoked strong reactions, with one local dance critic referring to it as "victim art" and refusing to attend any performances. In Europe, many choreographers address the issues of our troubled times using their own resources—bodies and dance. Lloyd Newson, a militant homosexual from Australia who moved to Britain where he founded the DV8 ["Deviate"] Physical Theater, explicitly deals on stage with the subjects of, among others, desire (*My Sex, Our Dance*) and homophobia (*Dead Dreams of Monochrome*). But Newson does so with extravagant imagination far removed from the somewhat deadly dull style of earlier "activist art." Colors and imagery abound, and when a legless dancer or an elderly woman joins the troupe, the audience realizes that it not simply a question

of provocation. In France, Alain Buffard's *Good Boy* raised the issue of illness by making high heels from medicine boxes, stuck directly to the dancers' feet. Rachid Ouramdane's *Loin* (Far) recounts the story of his father, an Algerian who enrolled in the French army during the war in Indochina. The rebellious duo of Héla Fattoumi and Éric Lamoreux, meanwhile, mocked the cult of body building in *1000 départs de muscles* and addressed the issue of the Islamic headscarf in *Manta* (2009). In Brazil, Lia Rodrigues and the Membros group (which started with hip hop) explore issue of the favelas (shantytowns) and the future of their youngest inhabitants.

Another crucial issue is collective memory: where have we come from, where do we find ourselves? Today's dance redraws the borders—a company such as the Lyon Opera Ballet, whose repertoire ranges from neoclassical ballet to contemporary dance, has members representing seventeen different nations! As a guest choreographer there in 2007, Ouramdane devised a piece called *Stars* to invoke these artistic migrations with their wealth of hybridizations. Anglo-Bengali choreographer Akram Khan also epitomized globalization through his *Bahok* (2008): the extensive dance vocabulary of his nine performers (variously from China, South Africa, Korea, and Great Britain) ranges from classical to traditional and allows them to imagine a shared "home" through dance. Here Khan also underscores the importance of cell phones for these new nomads of the art world. Finally, the Flemish, with Alain Platel at their head, evoke with each new work a world in quest of meaning—and sometimes religion—where flags are burned and homes are abandoned in signs of personal as well as choreographic transformation.

In December 1989 Pina Bausch premiered *Palermo Palermo*, her major work of that season. At the beginning of the show, inspired by the city of Palermo in Sicily, a wall of bricks collapses. So less than one month after the fall of the Berlin Wall, in a single scene rehearsed before the real events occurred in Berlin, contemporary dance had said it all.

LEFT

Akram Khan,
Bahok (2008).
The Anglo-Bengali
choreographer
called on classical
and contemporary
dancers from Asia
and the West for
this new work set in
a departure lounge.

RIGHT

Alain Buffard, *Good
Boy* (1998).
High heels made of
medical bandages
and plastic cups:
a metaphor for
unwell bodies in
the age of AIDS.

BELOW

Lloyd Newson,
The Cost of Living
(2003). This
choreographic fable
by the DV8 company
denounced the
consumerism of our
ever-changing world.

PAGE 40
Pina Bausch, *Palermo
Palermo* (1989)
Prepared several
weeks before the
Berlin Wall fell,
this work featured
the collapse of a brick
wall—premonitory
as well as spectacular.

PAGE 41
Rachid Ouramdane,
Loin (Far, 2008).
The young choreographer
Ouramdane combines
personal recollections
of his mixed background
with strong visuals that
include video projection.

IT CULTIVATES VARIETY

Dance often gives the impression of liking order: a ballet and its plot usually hinge on a pair of leading dancers (variously called principal, star, or guest dancer), a few more or less defined secondary roles, plus a corps de ballet that supplies the bit parts and extras. This "pyramidal" organization has the advantage of presenting the audience with a clear picture of things. But contemporary dance—among others—looks at things from a different point of view. As we shall see.

Even though the postwar years seemed to represent a radical break in choreographic practice, one thing remained unchanged: the emphasis on a star dancer, distant heir of prima ballerinas and premier danseurs. Maurice Béjart featured Jorge Donn, while Martha Graham had herself (plus a newcomer named Merce Cunningham). But the rise of postmodern dance in the United States led to a rejection of even this vestige of tradition: henceforth the group was more important than the individual, so a troupe spirit would replace star billing. This did not mean, however, that one kind of "obscurantism" was being replaced by another; when the performers' names appeared in the program, they were listed alphabetically rather than according to their rank in the company. **Choreographers began conceiving roles not for a single dancer but for a community of performers, although this did not prevent them from devising made-to-measure steps when inspired by a given dancer's personality.** What this new organization in fact permitted was the increasing presence of amateur performers with no specific dance training. Jean-Claude Gallotta founded the Groupe Émile Dubois in the late 1970s precisely on the principle of recruiting people from various backgrounds. Himself a self-taught dancer—having performed his first solo at the venerable age of twenty-two—Gallotta was a child of the revolutionary events of May 1968 and almost certainly viewed dance as a shared attitude rather than shared egos. He would constantly employ the metaphor of "tribe" in his works, filling the stage with children and, later, senior citizens (*Trois générations*, 2004). He referred to "the democracy of the eye" when discussing ballets that resembled the audience in its diversity. **By subverting the sole criterion of virtuosity, contemporary dance brings to the stage a variety of roles, some of which transform awkwardness into an asset.**

ABOVE
Jean-Claude Gallotta, *Trois générations* (Three Generations, 2004). Gallotta brought together on stage a children's troupe (Groupe Grenade), his own dancers, and a group of senior performers.

FACING PAGE
Frédéric Flamand, Ballet National de Marseille, *Métapolis* (2000). This ballet, a collaborative effort with the architect Zaha Hadid, is also an installation.

ABOVE

Dominique Boivin,
*Transports
exceptionnels*
(Unusual Load, 2005).
Operatic airs
accompanied this
outdoor duet, a love
affair between
man and machine.

Despite this situation, the opening of dance schools such as the Centre National de Danse Contemporaine (France), the Laban Center (England), and P.A.R.T.S (Belgium) meant that contemporary dancers could attain unprecedented levels of competence. Conservatories of dance in cities like Paris and Lyon further supply an entrée into contemporary dance. **These days it is rare to come across weak performers in a contemporary show. Which means that choreographers can take a lot of liberties—there are countless ways to dance, all different!** In certain cases, one good trick is to foil the dancing partner's expectations. The debut of the dazzlingly talented Belgian choreographer Wim Vandekeybus, *What the Body Does Not Remember*, which made a splash in 1987, involved a ballet of bricks that the company juggled at high speed. In between each toss they executed supercharged dance moves with urgent expressiveness and display. Frédéric Flamand, a Belgian who has headed the Ballet National de Marseille since 2004, takes mischievous delight in setting his nicely modern choreography in structures commissioned from architects and designers—thus Jean Nouvel, the Campana brothers, and Zaha Hadid have all supplied mobile sets and gangways that the dancers must come to terms with (not without risk). The confrontation with such obstacles lends additional reality to the choreography. The German troupe Neuer Tanz (New Dance), headed by VA Wölfl, goes so far as to deconstruct the performance itself—*Revolver* placed a clutch of secretaries in an "arty" set of neo-military tanks and inflatables, while *Das Chrom+Du* obliged his troupe to slalom among a collection of LP records to an extremely loud soundtrack that was a trial for both dancers and audience alike!

One of the cleverest challenges to conformism—to which even the most contemporary of arts is susceptible—was perhaps made by *Transports exceptionnels* (Unusual Load), choreographed in 2005 by Dominique Boivin for dancer Philippe Priasso. This pas de deux between dancer and full-size mechanical shovel revealed a wealth of imagination and delicacy. It was a love affair between man and machine—with humor thrown in. The dance was unaffected, which is precisely why it worked.

FACING PAGE

Frédéric Flamand,
Ballet National
de Marseille,
Métamorphoses
(2007).

Here Flamand
worked with Brazilian
designers Campana,
who contrived
the plastic set.

IT COMBINES SEVERAL KINDS OF ART

Gone are the days when dance was just movement through space. Contemporary dancers undergo protean training—they cultivate split personalities as singers and dancers, soloists and actors. Which is probably just another way of breaking down borders and mixing genres.

Where previously it was opera that sought the status of "total artwork," it might now seem as though contemporary dancers try to be "total artists." Without going back as far as Loïe Fuller (1862–1928), who devised her own dances, did her own lighting, and even filed patents for her choreographic inventions, it is obvious that the great upheaval of modern—then contemporary—dance called for multifarious performers. In the 1920s Germany pioneered the development of Tanztheater, which combined dance and the dramatic arts, a concept that would survive in various forms, notably when reinvigorated by Pina Bausch. In fact, members of her company speak lines as much as they dance. Maurice Béjart also had his dancers deliver lines, a trend that has increased with the new generation of contemporary choreographers. Thus it is not rare for audiences to feel, during a performance, that they are witnessing much more than a dance piece. Take Sidi Larbi Cherkaoui's *Foi* (Faith) and *Myth*, in which he combines actors and dancers, shifting from one realm to the other until, at the end, everyone begins singing traditional songs. So is it still dance? Yes. And is it more than dance? Of course. Choreographers from the Flemish school (Alain Platel, Koen Augustijnen, Hans van den Broeck, and Wim Vandekeybus) have no qualms about adding heat to this melting pot of performing arts. At the opposite extreme of—and in a lighter tone than—dance based on actual personal experience, José Montalvo and Dominique Hervieu combine dancers from various backgrounds (hip-hop, African, classical, contemporary) with actors and even clowns. Describing their aesthetic stance as "ultra-contemporary baroque," they are comfortable with the music of both Jean-Philippe Rameau and George Gershwin, despite the centuries that separate the two composers. Meanwhile, Régine Chopinot was known for her timely, fashion-conscious pieces until she met land artist Andy Goldsworthy, with whom she devised *Végétal* in 1995, a piece whose ecological and artistic concerns were in advance of their times: an incessant parade of dancers carries branches onto the stage and creates an ephemeral vegetal sculpture there. Here we are dealing with a borderline zone between dance, performance, and the visual arts.

Contemporary dance pieces sometimes seem to be synonymous with "head over heels" and "pie in the sky." That's because circus acts are exploited by the some of the most rambunctious choreographers (Josef Nadj, Philippe Decouflé, François Verret) as a way of reappropriating movement. In exchange, some circus performers have joined dance companies, bringing a virtuosity that sometimes threatens to become vacuous even as it lends new scope to choreography. Keeping your feet on the ground is no longer a quality once gravity can be overcome—or temporarily tamed. It is only a short step from the circus to puppet theater, which certain choreographers have approached in their own, offbeat way. A duo composed of Gisèle Vienne (who graduated from a marionette school in Charleville-Mézières, France) and Étienne Bideau-Rey (a choreographer), made a splash in 2001 with *Showroom Dummies*, which entailed a strange ballet of studied poses between performers and life-size puppets. Vienne, subsequently working on her own, went on to create new pieces that weave an arousing universe which plays on fantasies and stereotypes: dance of—and for—adults, once again breaking new ground. **Marginal art can be major art.**

FOLLOWING PAGES
Sidi Larbi Cherkaoui, *Origin* (2008). Cherkaoui likes mixing things ups—here four dancers shared the limelight with an early vocal-music ensemble called Saraband.

LEFT
Alain Platel,
vsprs (2006).
A ballet inspired
by Monteverdi's
Vespers, un early
form of opera.

BELOW
Gisèle Vienne,
Jerk (2007).
Cowritten with
Dennis Cooper,
performed by
Jonathan Capdevielle,
Jerk is the story of
a serial killer that
combines puppets
with human
presence.

ABOVE
Sidi Larbi Cherkaoui,
Foi (Faith, 2003).
A singer himself,
Cherkaoui puts flesh
on a piece full
of music and wit.

RIGHT
Alain Platel, *lets
op Bach* (1998).
In Platel's quasi-
documentary piece,
musicians are present
on stage and
performers are
personally committed.

DANCE MYTHS

contemporary dance has nothing to show for itself
FALSE!

FACING PAGE

Merce Cunningham,
CRWDSPCR (1993),
Merce Cunningham
Dance Company.
A perfect example of
a Cunningham-style
foursome: face to
face, arms bent,
legs extended.

The still-young art of contemporary dance is sometimes the victim of pre-conceptions, one of the most common being that it has nothing to show for itself, apart from a few performers in tights on a dance floor—all colorless. Dreadfully dull. Well, it's time you changed your tune if you still associate classical ballet with tutus and toe shoes, and contemporary dance with tights and bare feet.

Even Merce Cunningham, known for the relative austerity of his sets and costume right from the start of his career in the 1950s, did not hesitate to call on fashion designers (such as Rei Kawakubo of Comme des Garçons and Romeo Gigli) and artists (Robert Rauschenberg, Andy Warhol, and, more recently, Italian architect Benedetta Tagliabue) in order to add another dimension to his choreographic work. In Cunningham's wake, many other extraordinary ventures transformed theaters into skyscrapers, enchanted forests, amusement parks, and so on. Little by little, set designers, stage directors, lighting designers, graphic artists, and sound designers have joined the ranks of contemporary dance, turning it into an art that can often claim to represent a "total artwork," obviously following the earlier tradition of opera yet remaining sufficiently innovative to inspire countless artists. It is no coincidence that the great "men" (*sic*) of contemporary theater include the name of the late Pina Bausch, a past master—alongside set designers Rolf Borzik and Peter Pabst—in the art of creating truly incredible worlds on stage. The danger, of course, is that the dance itself is upstaged. But here again the best choreographers have a ready response: movement brings life to a modulable set, or to a mountain of flowers, or to a giant hamster wheel (in Meg Stuart's *Replacement*). **Dance today can be highly spectacular, just as it can be resolutely minimal—it is up to you to choose your team.**

Above all, choreographers have managed to get the most out of new technology. They blithely place sensors on their dancers' bodies in order to reproduce, via computer, the movement on a screen and thereby impart another dimension to the action, simultaneously real and virtual. Video has also arrived in force, not to cannibalize dance but to offer it new horizons. Dance thus wins all across the board, constantly presenting audiences with the unexpected. There where, just a few years ago, audience reactions tended to be disenchanted, at the end of a show you now often hear enthusiastic comments—"I didn't know that's what dance was about!" or "What a blast!"

Dance has a distinct sense of theater and imagery, which is the felicitous "fault" of contemporary training that now tends to be multidisciplinary, from Mudra to P.A.R.T.S. Professional exchanges have also become fruitful: a choreographer or performer may assist a stage or opera director, then return to dance with new ideas. Further proof that contemporary dance has its own web of influences can be found in the fact that English rock star David Bowie included the leading Canadian dance couple, choreographer Édouard Lock and dancer Louise Lecavalier, in his Sound & Vision tour. Movement and dance thereby invaded the rock scene. For that matter, many figures in the dance scene have contributed to music videos (the French duo Bouvier/Obadia in a Patrick Bruel video, Philippe Decouflé in a Fine Young Cannibals video and a New Order video), to musicals, and to movies (Blanca Li appeared in the French film *Le Défi* [*Dance Challenge*]). **Dance is blossoming everywhere—and dance performances can be showier than many other types of contemporary art.**

DANCE MYTHS

Meg Stuart,
Replacement (2006).
Following other
extraordinary sets,
Meg Stuart and
Barbara Ehnes here
devised a rotating
box of a stage.

FOLLOWING PAGES
Angelin Preljocaj,
Les 4 saisons…
(The 4 Seasons, 2005),
Céline Marié, Lorena
O'Neill, Isabelle Arnaud,
Nagisa Shirai,
and Solène Hérault.
French artist Fabrice
Hyber designed
the mobiles for this
wonderful piece
of "chaosography."

contemporary dance is always highbrow
FALSE!

Apart from certain extremes, the number of contemporary choreographers who have reached an increasingly wide audience reveals that dance is not so hard to appreciate as people think. From Philippe Decouflé to Angelin Preljocaj, to take just two convincing examples, the new way of conceiving contemporary dance has shattered this preconception.

If we define "highbrow" as elitist, that is to say an attitude that favors an elite over ordinary people, then contemporary dance could stand justly accused. The few studies carried out on audiences show that people who attend dance performances are white, college-educated city dwellers. But the same is true for opera, theater, and art exhibitions. In fact, audiences should always be conjugated in the plural, for contemporary dance manages to cast a wide net. True enough, certain solos or subtle works are more likely to appeal to a smaller audience, but this audience is equally varied. In largely immigrant towns just outside of Paris, where many public theaters host performances of dance, the audiences are a mix of specialists, local residents, and young people of all stripes. The heavy media focus on hip-hop has attracted more spectators with few preconceptions, open to hybridization between urban trends and contemporary dance—there are many examples of choreographers who shift from one to the other, such as Montalvo/Hervieu, Mourad Merzouki, Bianca Li, and Bruno Beltrão.

Similarly, major media events—sometimes televised—have prompted new audiences to take a look at contemporary dance. From Alwin Nikolais in the United States in the 1960s to Philippe Decouflé in France in the 1990s (known not only for choreographing the opening and closing ceremonies of the Winter Olympics in Albertville but also for shows such as *Codex*, *Shazam!* and *Sombrero*), choreographers have attracted new spectators both young and old. In a nice twist, for that matter, Decouflé "studied under" Nikolais at the national dance center in Angers, France.

This permeability has not resulted in a loss of identity. It simply means that the language of dance has managed to become accessible without sinking into a stultifying universality. It's all a question of education. The lack—or inadequacy—of education in the arts in primary and secondary schools (and beyond) has had a detrimental effect on many fields. The comment that it is often hard to get people into museums applies equally to theaters. Free admission is not the only answer—above all, efforts have to be made to bring dance and its (future) audience together: schools have to make outings to the theater, troupes have to head into the streets with concrete events. **Contemporary dance is not elitist, it is simply little-known.** Preconceptions abound. A few figures can be revealing, even if quantity is not the only guarantee of quality: performing artists such as Decouflé, Montalvo/Hervieu, and Preljocaj have already toured the world and been seen by hundreds of thousands of spectators; Maguy Marin's *May B.* has been performed over 650 times; **the international dance biennial hosted by Lyon, France, boasts total attendance of eighty thousand, a figure that doubles during its outdoor dance parade. Yet at the same time, some choreographers unveil new works at venues that have only a few dozen seats, occupied by a clutch of dance enthusiasts. Highbrow? Not necessarily. Difficult? Sometimes. Rewarding? Always.**

Philippe Decouflé, *Sombrero* (2006). Christophe Salengro, a lanky actor who became a dancer (here partnered by Flavien Bernezet) lends his inimitable physical presence to Decouflé's work.

DANCE MYTHS

José Montalvo and Dominique Hervieu, *Un danSe* (We're DanCing, 2004). The choreographers imparted a new dimension to dance by playing on depth and projected imagery.

FOLLOWING PAGES
Alwin Nikolais, *Crucible* (1985), revived here by the Ririe-Woodbury Dance Company in 2004. A master of special effects as well as a choreographer, Nikolais employed mirrors to transform the body into pure movement—and color.

José Montalvo and Dominique Hervieu, *Paradis* (1997). A great mix of dance styles—African, classical, contemporary—translates into contagious energy on stage.

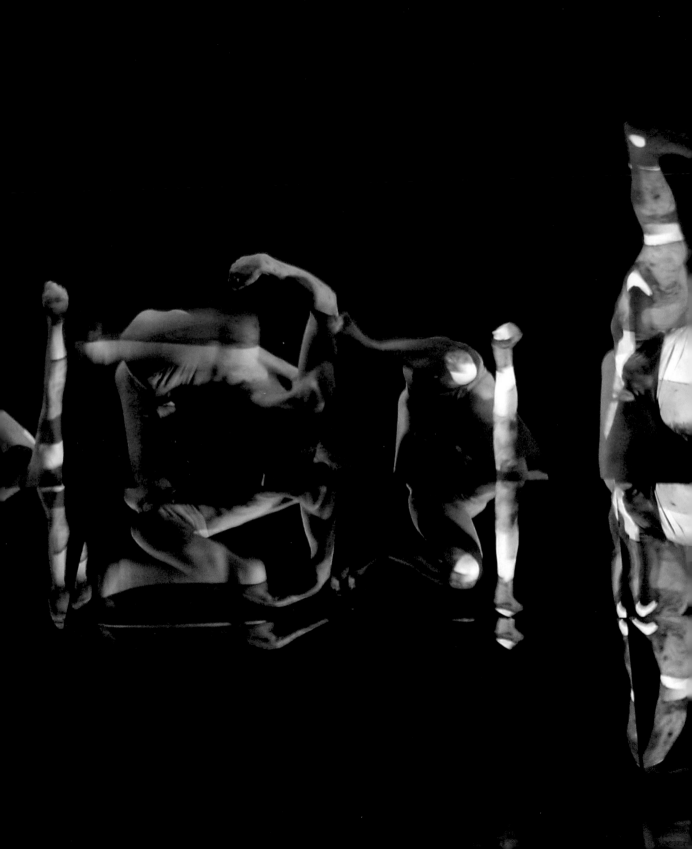

contemporary dance has no real stars
TRUE and FALSE!

The general public has become aware of a few dance "stars," such as Mikhail Baryshnikov, who even appeared in the TV series *Sex and the City*, or Patrick Dupond in France. It is perhaps more apt to refer to "hero worship" of figures from the world of ballet.

The arrival of contemporary dance coincided with the appearance of "real" bodies, that is to say that the person performing a role is also, and above all, a real individual. There is no longer a corps de ballet—that is to say a throng of minor roles—in which a dancer can hide. In contemporary dance performances, everyone is a lead dancer. Gone are the days when a haughty superstar refused to allow anyone else to dance a main role. In a piece commissioned by the Paris Opera Ballet, a maverick choreographer of the 1990s named Jérôme Bel featured Véronique Doisneau, a rank-and-file member of the classical company who, in this work named after her, described the "torture" of dancing in *Swan Lake* where she was just one of many swans, waiting for what seemed like forever before performing the briefest of variations. Choreographers who similarly reject the star ethic have begun emerging here and there. It would not be wrong to speak of "collective" performances, at the risk of alarming spectators who like leading roles (in the movies, theater, and elsewhere).

In short, there is an increasing number of excellent contemporary dancers yet fewer and fewer well-known names. Some dancer-choreographers have become icons, such as Carolyn Carlson (a poster girl in the dorms of sophisticated college students in France in the 1970s) and Pina Bausch. Béjart himself even admitted one day that his "job was to be famous"—he was often amused when a taxi driver could say, "Good Morning, Mr. Béjart," without knowing exactly what his profession was. **And yet even without a somewhat distant star like Sylvie Guillem, contemporary dance has produced several leading figures who now stand out in a crowd (if they are not exactly mobbed in the street by hordes of fans).** Louise Lecavalier, who performs the highly acrobatic pieces choreographed by her Canadian compatriot Édouard Lock, was certainly the brightest star of the 1980s, marking those years with her bleached white hair, muscular body, and physical prowess (especially her full-body barrel jump, that looked like a "horizontal" pirouette). Having briefly abandoned the stage due to injury, Lecavalier returned in top form to perform more

serene pieces. With *I is Memory*, by Canadian choreographer Benoît Lachambre, she once again asserted herself as an artist who mattered (at an age when others are already contemplating retirement). And certain members of Bausch's Wuppertal Tanztheater have also become stars of the dance world, such as Dominique Mercy (in his undone tutu) and Nazareth Panadero (with her throaty voice and frizzy hair).

Finally, this pantheon of performers must include Kazuo Ohno, the Japanese dancer who forged *ankoku butoh* ("dance of darkness," known in the West as Butoh) with

Kazuo Ohno, *Admiring La Argentina* (1977). Having emerged from the Butoh school of the 1950s, Ohno later invented this highly moving, ambiguously gendered character.

Tatsumi Hijikata. Ohno notably popularized a transvestite role, La Argentina, based on a Spanish flamenco dancer he once saw perform. Dressed in a long dress and hat veil, with white-powdered face, Ohno's character made an impact around the world and is today almost iconic—it resurfaced in 2009 on the cover of an album by angel-voiced singer Antony Hegarty (*The Crying Light* by Antony and the Johnsons). Ohno became a legendary figure in the contemporary dance world's collective imagination, dancing until he was over one hundred years old—he died on June 1, 2010, aged 103.

RIGHT
Pina Bausch,
Bandoneon (1980).
Dominique Mercy,
one of Wuppertal
Tanztheater's fetish
dancers, here parodies
a classical ballet
position—complete
with tutu.
FOLLOWING PAGES
Édouard Lock, *Infante
C'est Destroy* (1991).
Louise Lecavalier,
Édouard Lock's muse,
performs her famous
barrel roll. This is
dance on the edge.

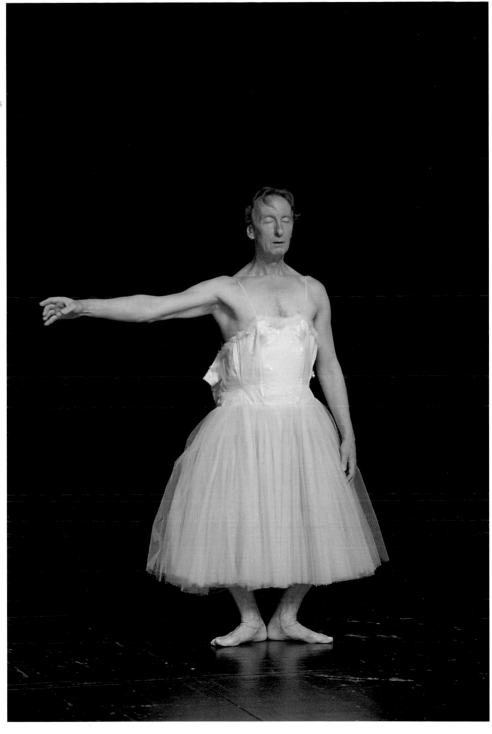

contemporary dance is performed by non-professionals
TRUE and FALSE!

A simple list of dance courses, schools, and conservatories should suffice to convince the most skeptical of observers of the quality of training offered to contemporary dancers. And yet some choreographers do not hesitate to break down the professional/amateur barrier by creating works that include roles for children, senior citizens, and people like me and you—especially you!

Given its iconoclastic origins, contemporary dance has always been open-minded. And open to a mingling of people and persuasions. Although the great of majority of performers and choreographers past and present have had traditional training—often through classical, modern, jazz, or contemporary dance courses or schools—other clever practitioners enjoy a different view of their art. Take the example of Jean-Claude Gallotta, from Grenoble, France. He started as an art student, then at age twenty or so he became hooked on tap-dancing and classical ballet. After training very briefly in the United States, Gallotta returned to France and founded the Groupe Émile Dubois, a "collective" in the broadest sense, some of whose members displayed an artistic sensibility but had never danced. Another fan of collective creativity is Alain Platel from Belgium, who came from a completely different background—he was an orthopedist who took care of children. While living in Ghent, he discovered his knack—despite a lack of any previous indication—for stage direction and choreography, and taught himself as he went along, convinced that dance was more than just Béjart. Indeed, dance was also Bausch, one of his first revelations when still a member of the audience. Platel's pieces, produced over a twenty-year career as head of a collective called Ballets C de la B (for Contemporains de la Belgique, i.e., Contemporary Ballet of Belgium) **have included not just terrific dancers but also circus performers, singers, and disabled people who at one point or another turn out to be surprising interpreters of movement. You don't have to train for ten years in order to dance!** Sidi Larbi Cherkaoui, a former fellow traveler with the Ballets C de la B, also strays from the beaten path. In *Ook*, choreographed for the Theater Stap in Belgium, he recruited mentally disabled actors for a series of improvisations around each actor's dreams. The result was not pathos, but a true lesson in life. For *Sutra*, Cherkaoui sought out Shaolin monks in China; on stage, they become acrobats, Zen philosophers, and dancers. According to Cherkaoui, his

goal was not to turn them into conventional performers, but to breathe a little dance into their physical discipline based on the martial arts. It worked beautifully.

But the person who went furthest in this non-professional direction was Pina Bausch with her Tanztheater. In 2000, she decided to revive *Kontakhof*, one of her key works, with performers aged over sixty-five—none of whom had dance training. Bausch later said that she did not have time to wait for her own dancers to age, in order imbue *Kontakhof* with a second life. So she placed ads. Dozens of senior citizens tried out (more women than men). Aided by Josephine Ann Endicott and Beatrice Libonati, her assistants and previous performers of *Kontakhof*, Bausch produced an extremely moving new version of the piece. Set in a dance hall furnished only with a piano, chairs, and a rocking horse, *Kontakhof* is a tale of contradictory feelings, sad dances, and groping waltzes. The non-professionals lent the performance an added dimension of personal experience. One of the "dancers," a widower who had lost his taste for most things, told Bausch that after the premiere he took up the piano again. Meanwhile, in 2008 yet another version was produced, this time with totally untrained teenagers from Wuppertal, chosen by tryouts. **The event was yet another miracle, as this occasionally hesitant and awkward *Kontakhof* made true performers out of kids who could have been anybody's brothers and sisters. It went straight to the heart of contemporary dance.**

FACING PAGE

Sidi Larbi Cherkaoui, *Sutra* (2008). Cherkaoui, alone on stage with Chinese Shaolin monks (including a young boy), engages in cross-border dialogue inside boxes designed by sculptor Antony Gormley.

FOLLOWING PAGES

Pina Bausch, *Kontakthof for Ladies and Gentlemen Sixty-Five and Over* (2000). Bausch revived her 1978 ballet with inexperienced seniors—to stunning effect. She repeated the experience in 2008 with teenagers.

DANCE MYTHS

contemporary dancers lack grace
FALSE!

The bodies that appear in classical, neoclassical, and modern dance all obey certain canons of beauty: a slender ballerina rises on a single toe shoe, a Béjart-style star dancer like Jorge Donn sweeps his perfectly shaped muscles and wavy hair through *Bolero*. It is a short step from there to the statement that contemporary dance is exactly the opposite—a step that won't be taken here.

Instead, suppose that contemporary dancers were simply a reflection of their times. That is to say, they are neither of the past nor the future, but truly of the present. Which represents another revolution. Indeed, the figure of a ballerina with toes turned inward, incredible posture, and perfect chignon is as representative of the modern body as is the rake-like silhouette of today's top models. In other words, an exception that proves the rule. By freeing itself from numerous rules, contemporary dance shows "us" just as we are all across the planet: in various sizes, skinny and fat—William Forsythe even used female dancers much taller than his men. And contemporary dancers may bear other marks of reality. Yet make no mistake, the ideal dancer is still someone with a broadly athletic physique, although performers such as Olivier Dubois and, more recently, Thomas Lebrun have turned their unusual physiques—with surplus pounds—into an asset. It is not so much Dubois's flab, as seen in Jan Fabre's *Histoire des larmes* (History of Tears) and Nasser Martin-Gousset's *Peplum* (Historical Epic), that is striking, as is the grace of a dancer who thumbs his nose at the dictates of a certain fashion. It is not *who* dances and *how* that is important, but *what* the dance conveys to the audience.

PAGE 72

Jan Fabre, *L'Histoire des larmes* (The History of Tears, 2005). By challenging the stereotypes associated with dancers' bodies, Fabre created a scandal when this piece premiered at the Avignon Festival.

PAGE 73

Olivier Dubois, *Faune* (2008). Dubois first came to attention when performing for Jan Fabre; here he pays a somewhat provocative tribute to Nijinsky's faun.

FACING PAGE

Philippe Decouflé, *Shazam!* (1998), Alexandra Naudet. Following the success of *Codex*, Decouflé made the big time by coordinating the opening ceremonies of the Winter Olympic Games. That event was followed by his ballet *Shazam!* which featured costumes by Philippe Guillotel.

In contrast, an artist such as Christophe Salengro, an actor by training who became a neo-dancer by force of circumstance, exploits his tall, gangling figure to bring a touch of lightness to the choreography of Philippe Decouflé, who recalls having first noticed Salengro at a party where he was dancing in his own special way, arms swinging above the rest of his body. Is Salengro ungraceful? Not really, he is just different, and that makes all the difference. By bringing to the stage all these ordinary—and, it should be noted, occasionally superb—bodies, contemporary choreographers are treating the audience as equals. Pursuing this idea, it might be said that educating the public eye also includes the representation of minorities, from African-American dancers to the children of immigrants. There where classical ballet tiptoes—on pointe shoes—contemporary dance has rushed straight in, getting in tune with today's multicultural society. In a movement begun on the West Coast of the United States in the 1960s, the tireless pioneer Anna Halprin was one of the first choreographers to assign roles indifferently to black and white dancers. That was a first big step. **There remained other obstacles and taboos, but starting from these little leaps contemporary dance has begun to advance in giant strides.**

DANCE MYTHS

classical ballet is an art, contemporary dance is a sport FALSE!

Abandoning narrative to the benefit of, among other things, abstraction, contemporary dance has often been charged by certain people with doing little more than gesticulating. Since there is no story, there is nothing to understand. Some commentators even mischievously refer to an artistic sport, aligning the new trends in dance with trends in aerobics and gymnastics. All that is missing are the ribbons and hoops.

As might be expected, the reality is a little more complicated. For that matter various sports—usually high level sports—have supplied their own battalion of dancers who soon specialized in the art either as performers or choreographers. Take Sylvie Guillem, the prima ballerina who left the Paris Opera Ballet and has now, aged over forty, reinvented herself as a modern dancer; a highly gifted gymnast, Guillem could probably have opted for an Olympic career. She even said that when she first arrived at the Opera ballet school she was treated like a freak. Performers currently in the limelight, such as Pierre Rigal from France and Emanuel Gat from Israel, were also athletes before turning to dance. And yet anyone who has seen their work (*Érection* and *Press* by Rigal, *The Rite of Spring* by Gat) know that neither man has anything to prove when it comes to choreographic composition.

It is obvious that both professions share a quest for excellence, long hours of practice, and above all a very brief career. Performing artists abuse their bodies far more than do painters and poets. It is hard not to think of Sylvie Guillem, after a performance of *Sacred Monsters* in London, begging leave of her guests so that she could go have her massage—which lasted an hour! Discipline worthy of an Olympic medalist. But dance—both classical and contemporary—indeed comes down firmly on the side of art, because in the end there is no medal, no prize, no podium. A dancer suffers pain alone, yet never forgets to share his or her pleasure with the audience.

You only need to count the number of actors and singers who have trained in dance—only to give it up—to understand the fascination associated with this simultaneously majestic and thankless discipline. "It should be said, over and over, that a dancer's life is a hard one," Mikhail Baryshnikov told this author not long ago. "And that it's always easier when you're the best in your field. Completely contented dancers are a rare breed indeed." Baryshnikov, the symbol of an intelligent performer, knows what he is talking about, having injured his knees like any other athlete. At which point he reinvented himself as a contemporary dancer—not just another career change, but a very sensible approach to his profession.

Above, contemporary dance has to come to terms with its times and its preconceptions. There where classical ballet swiftly established its system—hierarchy of roles, fairy-tale plot, and virtuoso execution, not forgetting its star system (Nureyev, Margot Fontaine, Pietragalla, Dupond)—contemporary dance has had to swim against the tide by rejecting pure performance in favor of anonymity and (relative) democracy on the stage. **And just as people always said of Picasso, "my kid could do that," so people have said of masters like Cunningham, "I do the same thing—at home!" Yeah? Just try it.**

Pierre Rigal, *Arrêts de jeu* (Injury Time, 2006). Rigal's piece is based on a striking childhood memory: a semifinal soccer game between France and Germany in 1982. Sport is here an excuse for exploring the very nature of athletic performance, with a touch of wit in the oversized padding.

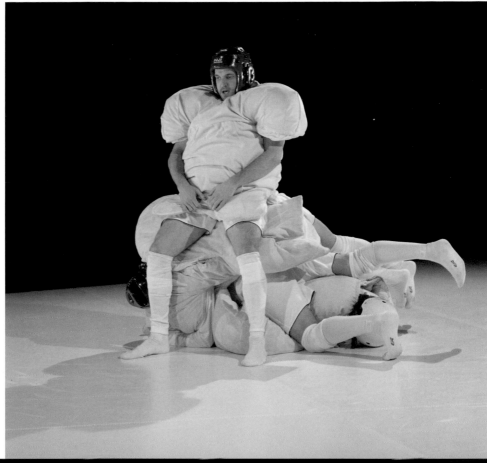

IF YOU LIKE...

IF YOU LIKE...

EROTICISM AND NUDITY

Jump straight in. When you think about it, nothing seems more obvious than a nude dancer. Yet anyone trying to get a glimpse of bare breasts in the early twentieth century would have been disappointed. Isadora Duncan was draped, while Nijinsky was covered in a leotard—and scandal. It would take time before dance stripped bare, before contemporary dance went erotic.

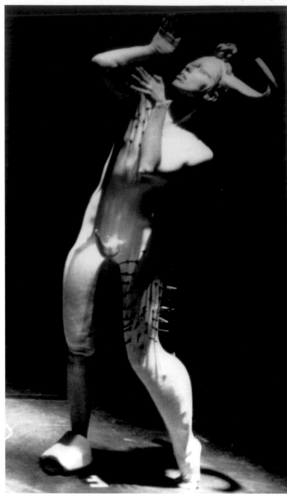

IF YOU LIKE . . .

ABOVE

Marie Chouinard, *L'Après-midi d'un faune* (Afternoon of a Faun, 1987). Chouinard looked to the original motif when conceiving her female faun with horns and other protuberances.

FACING PAGE

Angelin Preljocaj, *Near Life Experience* (2003).

The ambient eroticism of this work, to spacey music by the group Air, simultaneously reveals and veils the body.

The very title of Angelin Preljocaj's *Liqueurs de chair* (1988, Bodily Liquors) says a good deal about the (perhaps disreputable) intentions of this choreographic ringleader who continues to make audiences blush. Referring to "the sweet, heady substance that beads on the skin like sweat, sperm, blood, and tears," Preljocaj turned this ultra-modern ballet into an ode to highly sexed bodies, studding the stage with dancers in costumes of leather and other materials with deep cleavage. The highpoint of the piece was a kind of sex machine where the couples frolic. Since that time, Preljocaj has occasionally returned to his choreographic "obsessions" in classy productions such as *Near Life Experience* (with solo dancers in underwear and neo-bondage straps) and *Snow White* (with a stepmother who seems straight out of an S & M-oriented Japanese comic book). Preljocaj's very free tone has transformed dance into an extension of eroticism.

At the opposite extreme of Preljocaj's almost courtly manners, the protean and immodest Flemish artist Jan Fabre goes further still in a staccato idiom in which modern heroines wear armor, as seen in *Das Glas im Kopf wird vom Glas* (Glass in the Head Will be Made of Glass). More a visual artist than choreographer, Fabre's piece for solo dancer, *Quando l'uomo principale è una donna* (When the Principal Man is a Woman), was a tableau of nudity bordering on the fine arts; the female performer (a role created by Lisbeth Gruwez), totally nude, plays with vials of olive oil, which she empties drop by drop. Once slathered in oil, she daringly falls, glides, and rises again, all the while playing with Ben-Wa balls—and making the audience blush! In yet another piece, Fabre and his "warriors of beauty" evoke an *Orgie de la Tolérance* (Orgy of Tolerance) full of erotic undertones.

Meanwhile, choreographer Marie Chouinard went straight to the point of a totally different set of concerns in a series of explicit performances. Her *Petite danse sans nom* (Nameless Little Dance), in which she urinated on stage, was briefly banned in Montreal. Her interpretation of *L'Après-midi d'un faune* featured androgynous creatures sporting prosthetic genitals at their waist, like trophies of their manhunts. Chouinard also had panting dancers reinterpret

Orphée et Eurydice (Orpheus and Eurydice, 2009) in underwear, in a performance not suited to all ages yet not surprising from a choreographer who also presented
L'Amande et le diamant (Almond and Diamond), a solo piece
based on her interest in tantric tradition, the almond representing the vulva and the diamond symbolizing the penis.

Even if Anna Halprin pioneered this path back in the
1960s with nude dancers in "Paper Dance" (part of
Parades 8 Changes), she had few "heirs." Stephen Petronio,
who danced in Trisha Brown's company, played on gender mix with his partner of the day, English neoclassical
dancer Michael Clark, in pieces such as *Middle Sex Gorge*.
Meanwhile, Karole Armitage, the "punk ballerina" who
first made her mark in George Balanchine's company,
combines semi-pornographic imagery and pas de deux
in *Contempt*, and she also works with provocative artists
such as David Salle and Jeff Koons. In *Rave*, she had the
Ballet National de Lorraine parade by in costumes that
were as revealing of fantasies as they were of bodies.
Spanish choreographer Blanca Li might be a distant
cousin of this erotic family; in *Le Songe du Minotaure*
(Dream of the Minotaur) she arrayed bare-breasted but
waist-draped women as though they were aligned on a
conveyor belt. She was obviously evoking ancient Greek
statuary with its "uninhibited approach to nature and sex,
to philosophy and humor"—not to mention art.

Comfortable in registers as varied as hip-hop and modern flamenco, Li has recently gone further in a new piece
based on the garden of delights (*Le Jardin des délices*),
where "heaven mingles with hell, pleasure, and vice."
Heads up, hot stuff.

**It would be a shame to overlook a final realm in
which contemporary dance strips off—namely
striptease.** In *Belladone* (Belladonna), a great team of
contemporary choreographers—including Alain Platel, Wim
Vandekeybus, and Vera Montero—took a provocative
approach to undressing by reversing the erotic stance:
they turned the audience—voyeurs par excellence—into
actors in the show! As to Philippe Decouflé, he shifted from
minor mode (*Coeur croisé*, a romantic-style piece against
a striptease background) to major key by becoming,
in 2009, the art director of the Crazy Horse, the famous
Paris cabaret that turns nude revues into an art form.
**Contemporary dance will henceforth play a role
there—a maverick role, as usual.**

Jan Fabre, *L'Orgie de la tolérance* (Orgy of Tolerance, 2009). A peerless provocateur, Fabre denounces society's pretences, symbolized by these dildoed noses.

FACING PAGE (RIGHT)
Jan Fabre, *Quando l'uomo principale è una donna* (When the Principal Man is a Woman, 2004), a solo role created by a nude Lisbeth Gruwez, dripping in oil. A portrait of a sensual, arresting woman.

RIGHT
Sasha Waltz, *Körper* (Body, 2000). With its strong visuals—such as a glass box inhabited by dancers—*Körper* is an emblematic work by this German choreographer.

LEFT AND FACING PAGE
Blanca Li, *Le Jardin des délices* (The Garden of Delights, 2009). The Spanish choreographer expropriates Hieronymus Bosch's famous painting in a sometimes daring work based on cabaret theater and enlivened with moving images by Eve Ramboz.

MINIMALISM

If perpetual motion leaves you cold, if virtuoso pas de deux bore you stiff, and if vast choreographic frescoes are not your cup of tea, then you must be a fan of minimalism. Minimalist dance—or non-dance, as some people wrongly describe it—reflects upon, and frees itself, from standard codes. Its new deities are called Bel, Le Roy, Salamon, and Leroux.

LEFT
Jérôme Bel, *Nom donné par l'auteur* (Name Given by Author, 1994). The "choreographer" defines, on stage, the very nature of a "spectacle."

FACING PAGE
Eszter Salamon and Xavier Le Roy, *Giszelle*, second part (2001). An ironic look at the body of a ballerina.

FOLLOWING PAGES
Eszter Salamon, *Reproduction* (2004). A work about gender and identity, with female dancers dressed as men pretending to be women!

Is minimalism an authentic trend in dance? An affirmative answer is a risky one, yet it is clear that at various periods choreographers have rejected the completely dynamic, completely choreographed, completely danced ethic in order to explore another form of corporeal research. The figures associated with the New York's Judson Church Theater in the fertile 1960s dared to shake off the inhibiting mantle of the likes of Merce Cunningham, who himself had already abandoned the codes of classical ballet and the idiom of Martha Graham. Contact-improvisation (which focuses on increased points of contact between two people), performance art, protest actions, and daily tasks and rituals were all elaborated in various ways and various places by choreographers working with visuals artists, musicians, and filmmakers. Although the names of Steve Paxton, Yvonne Rainer, and Simone Forti are little known outside specialist circles, many young European choreographers still refer to them today, sometimes re-staging their pieces or inviting them as guests.

Trisha Brown was the only member of this movement to enjoy a broad international career, thanks to a number of compromises, such as founding her own company, performing in large theaters, and accepting commissions. **In the 1990s there was an apparent revival of minimalism by a wave of dancers, some of whom emerged from contemporary dance troupes, who then went over to "the other side."** Jérôme Bel typified this simultaneously formal and conceptual undertaking, which often turned out to be fascinating. The very titles of Bel's pieces such as *Nom donné par l'auteur* (Name Given by the Author) and *Jérôme Bel* set the tone: self-reflexiveness, introspection, and crisis of identity (or rather confirmation of the identity of the dancer-objects of the 1980s, who here became subjects). These undanced ballets said a good deal about the simmering crisis—one of Bel's performers listed the particular features of his body (from folds of flesh to overall weight) while another whistled the theme of *The Rite of Spring*.

Xavier Le Roy, meanwhile, began with a self portrait (*Narcisse Flip*) and then went on to zip his *Giszelle* [sic] into a shopping bag straight out of a discount mart; this latter piece also featured Eszter Salamon, a dancer who made her mark with Mathilde Monnier and François Verret, leading figures of the 1980s. Her *Giszelle* was a cousin to Madonna and Michael Jackson, except that her limited space forced her to rethink her movements. Later, as a full-fledged choreographer, Salamon would explore family relationships and troubling issues of gender, as seen in *Reproduction*, one of the most successful pieces by the disenchanted generation of the AIDS years. The audience flanked a vast stage on which were "reproductions" of stereotypes of uncertain gender, whose "dance" was composed not so much of movements as of a change of wig or a steady leer. Unsettling.

Other agitators, while not challenging the grammar of dance, advocate another kind of minimalism, based for example on a single dancer in a performance that includes philosophers, dog handlers, and former homeless people as was the case with Michel Schweizer's *Bleib* (Stay). Here Schweizer, with his varied background, was questioning the mechanisms of seduction and of pack behavior. But was it still dance? The question does not arise in quite those terms, because the art of choreography, whose point of departure is above all the body—rather than what is done with that body—long ago extended its fields of investigation. A body is staged, its immobility is studied, it is reconceived as a duet: in short, it is explored in the wide-open laboratory—in the guise of a theater—of forms and meanings. Another maverick, Brice Leroux, works in yet another vein, employing a subtle alchemy based on mathematics and poetry (*Gravitations–Quatuor* and *Quantum-Quintet*). Figures traced on the floor are repeated in an almost endless twirling movement, all in an enchanting halo of light. The effect is minimal even though the preparatory work tends toward the maximal. The dance—or what remains of it—perceived by the audience is totally hypnotic.

AUTEUR-CHOREOGRAPHERS

This category may seem intriguing: a choreographer is not supposed to be an author (*auteur* in French). Yet, like auteur film directors, certain figures on the contemporary scene in the past forty years have developed their own special vocabulary that becomes an identifiable style of "writing."

Make no mistake: apart from copycats, choreographers as a whole compose original works, sometimes under the influence of others, usually of their own invention. Lucinda Childs was one of the inventive types, revealing her talent in 1979 in a piece simply titled *Dance*, a hypnotically repetitive series of loops tending toward infinity, in unison with a score by Philip Glass. Having participated in Robert Wilson's epic opera, *Einstein on the Beach* (also scored by Glass), Childs grasped the mechanisms by which movement can be perpetually regenerated on stage. As a talented disciple of Cunningham—also an auteur in his own right, but one whose influence far transcends this category alone)—Childs managed to make her own, still highly respected, name.

Childs's colleague, Carolyn Carlson (who came to notice in the company of Alwin Nikolais, that magician of graphic and corporeal effects), was not to be outdone, becoming a choreographer who developed her own visual and physical poetry in a career that spanned Venice, Paris (the Groupe de Recherche Théâtrale at the Paris Opera), and northern France (now based in Roubaix). Carlson's signature style entails long movements with outstretched arms, a quest for a Zen-like vertically, and the "movement of souls," as she puts it. Highly marked by the decade of the 1970s, her idiom has recently taken on new color thanks to the collaboration of video artists and live musicians (*Blue Lady Revisited* and *Eau*). So much the better.

Dominique Bagouet was a hero of this approach in the 1980s, having launched the Montpellier Dance Festival, the largest of its kind in France. Trained as a classical dancer, Bagouet became a star in the late 1970s; his choreographic grammar is based on small leaps, refined movement, and a lavish series of gestures that might be described as "contemporary baroque"—a subtle revamping of the royal ballets of bygone era. His style triumphed in pieces such as *Déserts d'amour* (Deserts of Love), *Assaï*, *Le Saut de l'ange* (The Angel's Leap), and *So Schnell* (So Fast). Bagouet died in 1992, one of the dance world's first victims of AIDS, but his name lives on thanks to the archives known as Carnets Bagouet.

Jean-Claude Gallotta, who might also be considered a champion of "auteur dance," emerged during the same period. Gallotta has never strayed far from his home turf of Grenoble, France, where he now heads the Centre Chorégraphique. His trademark vocabulary, which he often embodies on stage, is constituted of precise elements such as bounding leaps, amorous abruptness, and repeated diagonal movements across the stage. As a prolific choreographer, he composes fresco-like ballets that combine amateurs and professional, children and senior citizens. Yet he almost never wavers from his meticulous compositional style with its almost pictorial sense of detail.

The conceptual dance trend that originated in the United States and has been highly fashionable since the 1990s has probably made many people forget the notion of "auteur choreography," deliberately or not. Yet there are still choreographers who seek their own "poetic language," including, at the time of writing, Cindy van Acker from Flanders, now living in Switzerland. Her "phrasing" finds expression through solo passages, based on much floor work (with head often glued to the ground), on explorations of tension and torsion, and on an intertwining movement generated by looping armwork. Van Acker's strangely titled solos are simultaneously fascinating and difficult (*Antre* [Lair], *Lanx*, and *Obvie* [Obvious], to name just a few), and are very moving in their rich complexity. Like writing with the body—a wonderful definition of auteur choreography.

FACING PAGE

Dominique Bagouet,
Jours étranges
(Strange Days, 1992).
A serious, nostalgic
work based on
improvisations to
music from The Doors'
Strange Days album.

Carolyn Carlson in
a tribute to Thomas
Erdos held at the
Théâtre de la Ville,
Paris (2004).
A leading figure of the
1970s dance scene,
Carlson's solos with
their elaborate effects
and distinctive arm
gestures translated
into highly expressive
dance.

FACING PAGE

Cindy van Acker,
Lanx (2008).
Dancer-choreographer
Van Acker sketches
lines as well as
movement, even
on the floor. Her
austere pieces display
a mysterious beauty.

FOLLOWING PAGES

Lucinda Childs, *Dance*
(1979) Ballet du Rhin.
Working with artist
Sol LeWitt, who did
the sets and film
for *Dance*, Childs
forged a vocabulary
of repetitive yet
graceful movements.

IF YOU LIKE . . . .

URBAN MOVES

Hip-hop has emancipated dance, turning theaters and festivals into new playgrounds. A glance at the worldwide map of urban dance reveals that the United States is the center of gravity, with a few satellites such as Germany and Brazil.

In the past thirty years there has been a noticeable rise in dancers who grew up in the ghettos—or are simply the children of immigrants. Not feeling at home in schools or dance courses, they occupied the empty space of the street. Their own street. One talented French dancer and choreographer, Hamid Ben Mahi, recounted in his solo *Chronic(s)* how he was the only "A-rab" student in a ballet class full of little white ballerinas, and how he was often left out since he did not quite fit the "bill" of a charming prince. From piece to piece Ben Mahi has managed to transcend clichéd turns, becoming a full-fledged hip-hop choreographer. Understandably, other dancers never even tried to take that route. In France hip-hop had to grow up on its own, or almost, but has now won recognition and is seen in venues worthy of its eminently popular status—shows of urban dance tour more widely than certain contemporary choreographers.

The most influential urban choreographer in France at the moment is Mourad Merzouki, born in the ghetto of Saint-Priest just outside Lyon. He has developed a style that hooks up with the circus and with contemporary dance, turning a wall into an excuse to have a ball, or a row of plastic cups into a yardstick of technical virtuosity (just try dancing over a glass of water, and you'll understand the prowess at work in *Agwa* [Water]).

Merzouki founded Accrorap with another fellow traveler, Kader Attou, who was recently named director of the Centre Chorégraphique in La Rochelle, France. In *PetitesHistoires.com* (Anecdotes.com) Attou combines recorded texts with free-style figures (swinging over a couch, for example) all the while evoking memories of his father, a simple factory worker. In fact, although this hip-hop rebel always makes his audiences laugh or dream, he also adopts a political stance. And yet these dancers (of whom far too few are female, alas) do not make demands so much as offer reminders—via the performing arts—of the world in which we all live.

On the other side of the planet, in Brazil, a generation of choreographers has been exploring this path since the 1990s, such as, most recently, Bruno Beltrão, and the Membros collective founded by choreographer Tais Viera

and political scientist and teacher Paulo Azevedo. The Membros collective dancers come from Macaé, usually from underprivileged neighborhoods. They use hip-hop like a weapon, employing speed and accuracy to express their hopes, all to the beat of samba funk. "We couldn't heal all the world's sorrows, so we decided to dance them," claimed Viera and Azevedo in the dance called *Febre* (Fever). In the United States, where the power of musicals still governs, there appears to be less urgency about exploring urban dance: a talented dancer like Doug Elkins focuses on floor work, head work, and swinging acrobatics that seem somewhat old-fashioned.

Finally, urban dance has won its stripes by contributing to the success of contemporary dance performances such as *Good Morning, Mr. Gershwin* by Montalvo/Hervieu and *Macadam Macadam* by Blanca Li. From street to theater is just a short hop—a hip-hop.

FACING PAGE

(TOP LEFT)
Kader Attou,
PetitesHistoires.com
(Anecdotes.com, 2008).
Attou came up with a
winning combination
of childhood memories,
circus techniques,
and hip-hop.

(TOP RIGHT)
Hamid Ben Mahi,
Édition spéciale (2001).
A dancer who briefly
flirted with classical
ballet, Ben Mahi
subsequently staged
his own work.

(BOTTOM LEFT)
Mourad Merzouki,
Agwa (Water, 2008).
The sole set of *Agwa*,
conceived in Brazil, is
a row of water-filled
plastic cups, which
the dancers address
with great skill.

(BOTTOM RIGHT)
Bruno Beltrão,
H3 (2008).
Floor work, lots of
hand and arm moves,
performers with great
presence: Beltrão gets
things right.

Membros, *Febre*
(Fever, 2007).
This Brazilian fever
is part of a hip-hop
trilogy on the theme
of violence in the
favelas (shantytowns).

Mourad Merzouki,
Agwa (2008).
Pared-down hip-hop
in shorts and knee
pads, a stack of plastic
cups in hand, and the
ever-present issue
of water (*agwa*).

FOLLOWING PAGES

José Montalvo and
Dominique Hervieu,
*Good Morning,
Mr. Gershwin* (2008).
Following their success
with the opera *Porgy &*

Bess, this pair of
choreographers
proposed a "danced
version" in which music,
video projection, and
hip-hop tell the tale.

Blanca Li, *Macadam
Macadam* (1999).
A summit meeting
between a modern

choreographer and hip-
hop dancers produced
this wildly successful
urban ballet with skate-
board set.

IF YOU LIKE....

AFRO-JAZZ & CO.

Afro-jazz, with its strong musicality based on jazz, swing, and Afro beats, knows the tune. A blend of various influences, from the rigor of classical ballet to the open-minded stance of modern dance, it is now enjoying a certain revival among the ghetto (and other) "kids" who grew up on hip-hop. So join the dance.

Jazz dance, a vague term covering a number of trends, has been under-appreciated by contemporary dance yet has remained fertile soil for much dance practice, if not choreographic invention. You need merely check out dance classes in places like New York, Montreal, Paris, and Lyon to see hundreds of amateur dancers sweating away at it. **Its energy and beat make jazz dance a vital activity.**

Alvin Ailey could be considered the mentor—and lead dancer—of the movement. The son of black farm workers, Ailey first attended a dance performance when the Ballets Russes de Monte-Carlo performed in Los Angeles. In Hollywood, he danced with Lester Horton and appeared in Otto Preminger's film, *Carmen Jones*. He furthered his training under Martha Graham, Doris Humphrey, and Katherine Dunham, that other great figure of black dance awareness. Ailey founded his own company in 1958, encountering early success with *Revelations*, choreographed to Negro spirituals. If expressiveness, a sense of theater, and the raw energy of African-American dance were to your taste, Ailey was your man! But in order to join his company or his classes, you had to brush up on your classics. Ailey, who claimed that "dance is for everybody," died in 1989, and was succeeded by Judith Jamison, who perpetuated his tradition by maintaining the repertoire and commissioning new works, formerly from Bill T. Jones, more recently from Camille A. Brown and Robert Battle. This jazz spirit is not the sole prerogative of African-Americans, however. Twyla Tharp could be said to have it. It's no coincidence that she worked for the Alvin Ailey American Dance Theater as well as the markedly more academic American Ballet Theater. Having trained in the Cunningham technique, Tharp then danced with Paul Taylor, and she draws inspiration from the vitality of Broadway with its musicals and regiments of multi-talented dancers. Between 1978 and 1984 she worked on films such as *Hair, Ragtime*, and even *Amadeus*. In *Nine Sinatra Songs* (1982), the influence of ballroom dance was apparent. Meanwhile, a minor masterpiece like *The Upper Room* (1986) is a supercharged compendium of incessant

dance movements as technical as they are devilishly fluid: beginning in academic white costume and bright red toe shoes—perhaps a tribute to Michael Powell's film *The Red Shoes*—the ballet progressively takes on other colors thanks to striped costumes by designer Norma Kamali. *The Upper Room* could be seen as an intellectual version of the film *All That Jazz* by Bob Fosse, the lord of Broadway musicals. It should perhaps be pointed out that in America artistic boundaries, while marked, are not rigid—members of the New York City Ballet love taking a look at what is happening on Broadway. In fact, Jerome Robbins, who succeeded company founder and director George Balanchine, worked in the movies, notably on *West Side Story*; and soon the New York City Ballet was advertising a *West Side Story Suite* alongside its usual numbers danced in tutus.

Finally, it could even be said that a choreographer like Karole Armitage, the former ballerina turned punk rocker, reflected the neo-jazz spirit in *Rave*, her piece for the dancers of the Ballet National de Lorraine. It is an ode to the often Latin-American heroines of "Voguing," so

Alvin Ailey, *Revelations* (1960). Ailey's powerful, athletic, and graphic choreography emblematized "black" dance in the 1960s.

fashionable in the 1990s. On stage they mime the poses of models for *Vogue* magazine. Even Madonna—who learned a great deal by attending Martha Graham classes—was influenced by voguing, and Armitage paid tribute to this minor yet flamboyant trend. And what could be said of a startling talent like Savion Glover, who took tap-dancing lessons? That he's a genius of timing, of course.

A range of names have done honor to the jazz spirit, from Rick Odums to Bruno Agati via Wayne Barbaste and Geraldine Armstrong. They are not only choreographers, but also remarkable teachers. If we extend the concept of jazz, it might be said that a contemporary-style chore-ographer such as Nasser Martin-Gousset is not so distant from the neo-jazz feeling; after just a few pieces, he has demonstrated a rare musicality, dancing to Nina Simone and to Dave Brubeck's (white!) jazz in *Comedy*. Finally, hook-ing up with hip-hop, Martin-Gousset's *I Want You*, chore-ographed for young dancers, is a remarkable interpreta-tion of American soul inspired by singer Marvin Gaye. Another way of pursuing the movement. Because black is still beautiful.

RIGHT (TOP)
Nasser Martin-Gousset,
I Want You (2009).
Smooth dancers (some
of whom came from
hip-hop) move beneath
nightclub-like lights to
a song of the same
name by Marvin Gaye.

RIGHT (BOTTOM)
Nasser Martin-Gousset,
Comedy (2008)
A cinematic use of the
stage, to live jazz music.

PAGE 102
Twyla Tharp, *In the
Upper Room* (1986)
Ballets de Monte-Carlo.
Borrowing from jazz,
musicals, and academic
technique, Tharp
concocted an energetic
classic dressed in
costumes by Norma
Kamali.

PAGE 103
Karole Armitage, *Rave*
(2001), Ballet National
de Lorraine.
By painting bodies
and reappropriating
costumes, Armitage
paid a tribute to the
stars of "voguing,"
a dance that parodies
the poses adopted
by models in *Vogue*
magazine.

VIRTUALITY

If, paradoxically, you like the image of dance as much as dance itself, you have come to the right place. Now, thanks to computer-generated imagery, the virtual has joined the real on stage. These parallel worlds are now very fashionable among choreographers.

At first it was just a shadow, which seemed to glide among the dynamic video projections. But in fact the young Japanese dancer and choreographer Hiroaki Umeda was truly present on stage, playing at virtual twins. In several solo pieces Umeda has revamped optical illusions and cinematic effects to contrive a dance infected with virtuality (*Adapting for Distortion, Accumulated Layout,* and *While Going to a Condition*). Amazing. In Japan, performing artists such as the theater collective Dumb Type and musician Ryoji Ikeda forged a multimedia approach that has opened the path to other young artists, including dancers. Once again, dance has become a multifarious activity thanks to the contribution of other arts.

The pioneer Merce Cunningham was doing just that when he decided to work with video artist Nam June Paik in the 1970s: the dancers performed in front of a wall of TV sets. Years later, in *Biped*, Cunningham turned to the team of Paul Kaiser and Shelley Eshkar, artist-researchers in the realm of virtual worlds. This time, more sophisticated technology made it possible to place sensors on the dancers' bodies, which dispatched data to a computer. Thus graceful silhouettes, recreated through technology, were superimposed on a screen placed in front of the dancing troupe—a lesson in composing poetry from electronic components. Cunningham was a pioneer in everything, keeping on the cutting edge of technology as well as keeping in touch with other artists (designers, composers, visual artists). Thus the choreographer sought new forms of movement by using DanceForms software; although he argued that nothing could replace studio rehearsals, Cunningham allowed himself to conduct virtual experiments that may—or may not—translate into dance steps. The wonderful thing about contemporary dance is that it does not have (many) preconceived notions about working with any other art.

Richard Siegal first made his mark as a dancer in William Forsythe's company, then moved to the other side of the choreographic looking glass. His solo *Stranger/Stranger Report*, with Sophie Laly at the video controls, questions our perception of theatrical representation in a bag-of-tricks installation from which the dancer suddenly appears or disappears as images and sounds interact with his bodily movements. Siegel also requires the audience to sign a release form, since the performance may be rebroadcast live thanks to hidden cameras.

When does the fake become real? This fuzzy distinction is frequently exploited by choreographers interested in virtuality. Swiss choreographer Nicole Seiler, for instance, in her fine *Ningyo*, projects fish scales onto her female dancer; as this mermaid-dancer multiplies, the audience is thrust into the murky waters of dance in the thrall of video. Belgian choreographer Karine Ponties, meanwhile, also employs touches of digital tech inspired by dance—and vice versa. In *Holeulone*, a male duo dancing on an inclined plane with openings is joined by a third partner in the form of projected images. The idea of "entering the picture" is not just a brilliant one, it also says a lot about current issues of the dematerialization of movement. Ponties furthermore works with another Belgian artist, Lawrence Malstaf, who is interested in the same issues. Meanwhile, a former athlete, Pierre Rigal, came to the fore with *Érection*, a solo piece in which he evolves from a horizontal position to a vertical one, thereby recapitulating human evolution; between those two extremes the dancer "goes through" walls of projections and a kaleidoscope of lights—an entire world is invented before the audience's eyes. The same is true of the shadow theater and other giant imagery devised by choreographer Philippe Decouflé and his assistant and performer, Olivier Simola; in *Sombrero*, the body is manipulated through screens, while the shadow theater-like shapes stretch on endlessly. **There is just time enough to realize that in fact it is a film being projected. Dance once again vanishes into thin air.**

ABOVE

Pierre Rigal,
Érection (2003)
A man stands up—
the "erection" of the
human race through
evolution—in a visual
environment of color
and images.

RIGHT

Hiroaki Umeda,
*Accumulated
Layout* (2007).
In this solo Umeda
adopts light as his
partner, intensifying
shadows and moves.

FACING PAGE
Philippe Decouflé,
Solo (2003).
Alone on stage in
a confessional role,
Decouflé invented
clever twins
of himself.

RIGHT
Pierre Rigal,
Érection (2003).
Developed with
a contemporary
circus artist, Aurélien
Bory, *Érection* is also—
and above all—about
a physical approach
to choreography.

FOLLOWING PAGES
Philippe Decouflé,
Sombrero (2006).
Head over heels,
these projected
images (sometimes
filmed live) lend an
additional dimension
to dance.

DANCE THAT DANCES

Maybe you think that movement is everything, as did Martha Graham when she said, "Movement never lies." And in the jungle of contemporary dance's various forms, from dance-theater to minimalism and performance art, you may worry that your "favorite child" will get lost. Never fear, certain choreographers still swear by movement alone.

The eruption of so-called contemporary dance onto the cultural landscape did not sound the death knell of pure movement—far from it. Many choreographers who reject a neoclassical approach nevertheless promote dance that dances. Period.

Canadian Édouard Lock studied literature before making a splash in the 1980s with pieces with striking titles such as *Human Sex* and *Infante C'est Destroy*. **His choreographic language reinvigorated the pas de deux and revived ensemble dancing with the entire troupe on stage, in unison. There was little or no narrative, apart from the story told by the body.** Above all, Lock invented new figures such as the barrel roll in which the dancers seem to spin horizontally. Lock, with his mixed background (Moroccan mother, Spanish father) seemed to redraw the borders of movement. Subsequently, he has dabbled with toe shoes and explored imagery with varying success (*Amelia* and *Amjad*).

Briton Wayne McGregor boasts a classical background. He trained at the José Limon dance school, was commissioned by the Ballet Rambert, and is resident choreographer at the Royal Ballet. But he really made his name with his own company, Random Dance. He has become the golden boy of British dance (having also worked on the movie *Harry Potter and the Goblet of Fire* and the musical show *Kirikou*), and asserts his uniqueness by working movement over and over again. Every gesture is drawn out in a sequence of moves that have a recognizably classical origin yet have been remolded into a contemporary virtuosity. The audience's attention is fully occupied—even overloaded—by ultracontemporary music and sets composed of projection screens. McGregor's dance seems to dread a vacuum. From *Entity* to *Genus* (commissioned by the Paris Opera Ballet), this prodigious choreographer has confirmed his heady talent.

Emanuel Gat, an Israeli living in France, might be considered a kid brother to the above choreographers. With an athletic background, Gat first discovered dance at the age of twenty-three. In just a few works, including a highly spiced *Rite of Spring* danced as though it were a salsa lesson, he has squarely placed movement at the center of his choreographic concerns. He describes *Variations d'hiver* (Winter Variations), a duet he performs with Roy Assaf, as a "zoom-in," as though his choreographic skills were combined with those of "movement editor" in a quasi-cinematic approach to dance. Hofesh Schechter has followed in Gat's footsteps to a certain extent, being another Israeli in Europe (London) who is becoming an international idol. After having trained at Batsheva, the leading Tel Aviv dance company and school headed by Ohad Naharin (who favors a physical approach to the art), the young Schechter, already a dancer and percussionist, choreographed two works, *Uprising* and *In Your Rooms*, **which feature much floor work, group work, contagious energy, staccato rhythms, and lively movement.** Schechter has only one desire: to dance. And to make others dance.

In a way, that is just what Garry Stewart from Australia wants. Pushing the members of his company onto the international stage, he has boldly created pieces that include robots (*Devolution*) and a distressing version of that Romantic classic par excellence, *Giselle*, in which the dancers, as though caught on a conveyor belt, file across the stage at top speed, replaying the story and passion of Giselle. Stewart's dance does more than just dance, it comes alive.

Dance dances in France, too, for the conceptualists and the theatrical crowd have not monopolized every venue. Inspired by Claude Brumachon and Jean-Claude Gallotta (both of whom have left behind their early indulgence in lyrical naturalism), several young upstarts including Abou Lagraa and Yuval Pick are carving out a bright future for themselves. That is to say, a whole new movement.

RIGHT

Édouard Lock, *Amjad* (2007). Although a contemporary choreographer, Lock dares to use toe shoes to lend a new virtuosity to his moves. PAGE 112

Emanuel Gat, *Variations d'hiver* (Winter Variations, 2009). Partnered by Roy Assaf, Gat devised a calligraphic dance with pas de deux and lifts conjugated in the masculine. PAGE 113

Wayne McGregor, *Genus* (2007), Benjamin Pech and Marie-Agnès Gillot. Commissioned by the Paris Opéra Ballet, *Genus* features poetic precision.

AFRICA

A whole continent of dance—that is what Africa is becoming, right before our eyes. From north to south, borderlines are shifting and new approaches are emerging, free from excessive influence. Creative performers are making their mark, exploring new horizons. Africa, fantastica!

Since the mid-1990s, the emergence of a whole generation of dancers and choreographers from Africa has become an indisputable fact as Robyn Orlin, Salia Sanou, Seydou Boro, Heddy Maalem, Kettly Noël, Taoufiq Izeddiou, Opyo Okach, and Faustin Linyekula have forged contacts with the rest of the world. They have also defined a "local dance" that is impossible to categorize, because it is multifarious, itinerant, adventurous. Germaine Acogny was a forerunner, then key figure, of this movement, serving in a way as a mother figure to the younger folk. A dancer and author (she wrote a reference work on the subject, *Danse Africaine*, in 1980), Acogny opened the first dance studio in Dakar, Senegal, in 1968. As a friend of Maurice Béjart, who had a Senegalese ancestor, Acogny piloted Béjart's Mudra-Dakar project as dancer and choreographer from 1977 to 1982; the Dakar branch was an African version of Béjart's Mudra school in Brussels. Then in 1999 Acogny opened the Centre International de l'École des Sables, where she kept her pulse on the new wave of dance rising in Africa. Salia Sanou pays affectionate tribute to Acogny by comparing to her a baobab tree.

There are more and more new talents appearing in Africa despite the difficult conditions (culture is rarely a priority for current governments). The continent enjoys strong links with France, either via exchanges (such as those made by choreographer Mathilde Monnier) or institutional support (a choreographic symposium for Africa and Indian Ocean countries has been held since 2000). **The main thing, however, is Africa's creative drive.**

South Africa, despite its history, has paved the way. Two of the country's most influential talents lived through the apartheid system and its fall, namely Robyn Orlin and Boyzie Cekwana (the latter having finally taken up dance again). In her pieces, Orlin—a white woman in a largely black land—evokes the stench of racism and cheaply bought clear consciences all the while denouncing, sometimes a little heavily, the mirage of a not-so-egalitarian society. *Daddy, I've Seen this Piece Six Times Before and I Still Don't Know Why They're Hurting Each Other* (1999) and *We Must Eat Our Suckers with the Wrapper On* (2001) typify her "mad" style

in which song and video share the stage with dance. In her wake, Nelisiwe Xaba and Via Katlehong (a troupe of township youths) have pointed in other directions. Xaba criticizes the condition of women while wrapping herself up in a cheap shopping bag (*Plasticization*, 2005) while the latter dance in the rubber boots worn by black miners even as they dream of a different world (*Woza*, 2008).

Political and social commitment motivates many new talents. Faustin Linyekula devises cabarets in which dance is combined with accounts of war. In *Le Festival des mensonges* (Festival of Lies, 2005), Linyekula, originally from the Democratic Republic of Congo (formerly Zaire), deals with his dead friends and the difficulty of doing creative work in a land in upheaval. Above all, Linyekula is open to other fields (he directed a production of the classical French play *Bérénice* and has worked on texts, *The Dialogue Series*, for his company, Studios Kabako). Serge Aimé Coulibaly from Burkina Faso, meanwhile, reflects the energy of Belgian choreographers, having worked with Alain Platel; *A Benguer* (The Other Side) shows young people left to their own devices, with uncertain future—should they flee the country to seek the European dream or should they stay and try to rebuild? Coulibaly's choreographic vocabulary, based on ground movements and influenced by urban dance, carries a lot of punch. Taoufiq Izeddiou from Morocco started his own company after having danced alongside French choreographer Bernardo Montet. Izeddiou's *Ataba* (2008) is a veritable cataclysm—the choreographer claimed he had only questions and a desire to "blow up the unknown." Worth following.

More consensual, perhaps, is the Burkina Faso team of Salia (Sanou) and Seydou (Boro), who not only work as choreographers but also founded the Centre du Développement Chorégraphique in Ouagadougou. In what is probably their most ambitious work, *Poussières de sang* (Flecks of Blood, 2008), **we find once again a physical vocabulary anchored to the ground (when not climbing onto one's partner's back, or rolling on the floor, or knocking against a wall). Usually accompanied by live musicians, Salia and Seydou are indebted to no one—African dance has finally come of age.**

Nelisiwe Xaba,
Plasticization (2005).
A political yet witty
solo, *Plasticization*
dresses its dancer-
choreographer in
a single toe shoe
and a shopping bag.

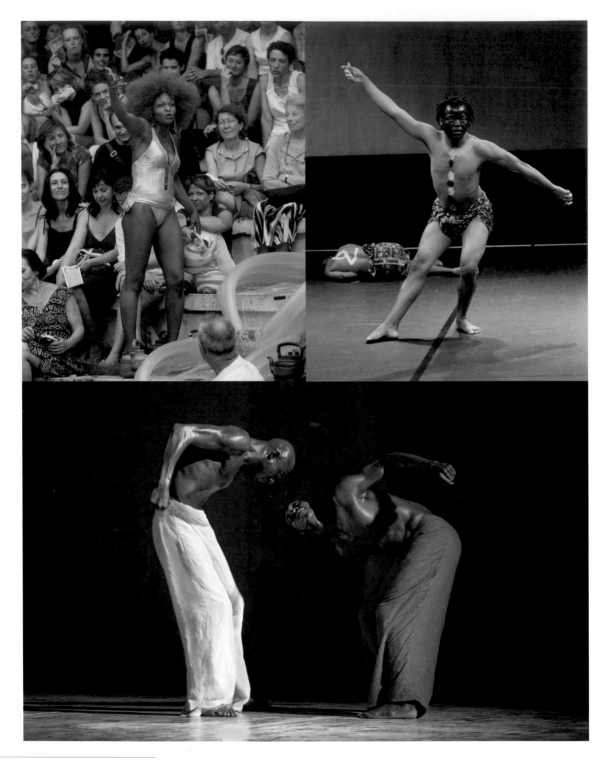

FACING PAGE

[TOP LEFT]

Robyn Orlin, *Although I Live Inside ... My Hair Will Always Reach Towards the Sun* (2004). A playful yet provocative solo performed by Sophiatou Kossoko, who doesn't hesitate to address the audience directly.

[TOP RIGHT]

Faustin Linyekula, *Dinozord: The Dialogue Series III* (2007). The socially concerned Linyekula combines dance, concert, and theater in an open-ended form.

[BOTTOM]

Salia nï Seydou, *Poussières de sang* (Flecks of Blood, 2008). Musicians and dancers jointly explore, with unusually evocative power, the tragedies that live within all of us.

RIGHT

Kettly Noël, *Chez Roselle* (2008). Haitian-born, Mali-based Kettly Noël explores a dance that is equally critical of blacks and whites.

FOLLOWING PAGES

Heddy Maalem, *The Rite of Spring* (2004). Born in Algeria, currently living in Toulouse, Maalem won recognition with a powerful interpretation of the *Rite* that featured fourteen African performers.

ASIA

If you like exotic trips with lots of Asian-style sensory input, then fasten your seat belts. Performing artists in Japan, China, Vietnam, and India will challenge your entirely Western preconceptions. Contemporary dance, thriving in Tokyo if still fledgling in New Delhi, is discovering new lands. Welcome to a voyage of discovery.

Rich in age-old traditions, many Asian countries still perpetuate their history through performing arts that were once highly codified. And why shouldn't they? Theatrical forms in which dance is more or less present—bharata natyam and kuchipudi in India, Bunraku, Noh and Kabuki in Japan, opera in China—**provide worldwide audiences with guaranteed exoticness. But it would be too limiting to stop there. These countries have changed or are changing, and are up-and-coming—when they haven't already arrived.**

Japan has experienced numerous artistic revolutions, of which Butoh* is one. Founded by talented, driven performers such as Tatsumi Hijikata and Kazuo Ohno, this "dance of darkness"—halfway between inner meditation and outer performance—produced a generation of heirs who have explored new paths, notably Ushio Amagatsu (from the Sankai Juku troupe), Carlotta Ikeda, and Saburo Teshigawara. Butoh's hallmarks are extreme stylization, theatrical gestures, and nearly naked bodies sometimes powdered white, often framed by spotlights. Amagatsu's sets are frequently spectacular, such as the wall of prints in *Shijima* and the hanging flowers in *Kagemi*, lending his pieces a neo-Butoh feel. Ikeda, henceforth based in Bordeaux, France, uses the grotesque to feminist ends while Teshigawara's formalist, visual experiments entail meticulously composed Zen choreography. Teshigawara has even danced on shards of glass (*Glass Tooth*) and a patch of grass; in *Miroku* he performed solo in a set of pure light. Following in these choreographers' footsteps is a new generation with a sophisticated Japanese vision—Kim Itoh's *KinJiki Forever!* features a highly sexed pas de deux for two men, while the young Hiraoki Umeda's *Accumulated Layout* is a solo piece with up-to-date video technology.

When it comes to China, given its tradition of folk dances and classical ballet (heavily Russian-influenced, even if local themes were injected into ballets such as *The Red Detachment of Women* and *Raise the Red Lantern*), everything has had to be reconceived from scratch. Contemporary dance by a performer such as Wen Hui looks at lasting social wounds (his duet *Memory* evokes the losers of the Cultural Revolution). Censorship still being very present in China, these choreographers finance their productions in Europe in order to maintain a relative autonomy. The often-invaded socialist republic of Vietnam, meanwhile, probably doesn't have the resources to finance an entirely new wave of dancers—one of the leading figures of the local scene, Ea Sola, has produced pieces such as *Sécheresse et pluie* (Drought and Rain) and *Il a été une fois* (Once Upon a Time) that evoke a land caught between reminiscence and modernity. Her timeless yet forward-looking works include traditional musicians and aging amateurs as performers. French choreographers such as Jean-Claude Gallotta and Régine Chopinot have made trips to Hanoi and Hue in an effort to encourage artistic exchanges with Vietnam.

Other lands, other companies: the Cloud Gate Dance Theater (Taiwan) and Legend Lin Dance Theater (Taipei) adopt a powerfully visual approach related to choreographic ritual, sometimes inspired by Taoism. Yet Asia's choreographic future will probably also be rooted in India, the world's largest democracy. Contemporary art has already set an example, although it is not certain that dance will enjoy the same success, at least not for the moment, due perhaps to the popularity of the eminently all-music, all-dancing film industry known as Bollywood. Yet a non-traditional choreographer like Padmini Chettur has devised very delicate pieces; in *Paper Doll*, dancers move like a chain of paper cutouts, whereas in *Pushed* the movement is based on a domino effect, one performer knocking over another, each gesture triggering an echo reaction. Shantala Shivalingappa is a well-known dancer of kuchipudi (one of the six main forms of classical Indian dance) who gracefully escaped tradition to dance with Maurice Béjart and Pina Bausch. Her recital of solos, called *Namasya*, **is a voyage through movement that presents another, highly contemporary, angle on creative dance. One that should whet your appetite for distant horizons.**

* See key words, p. 137–39

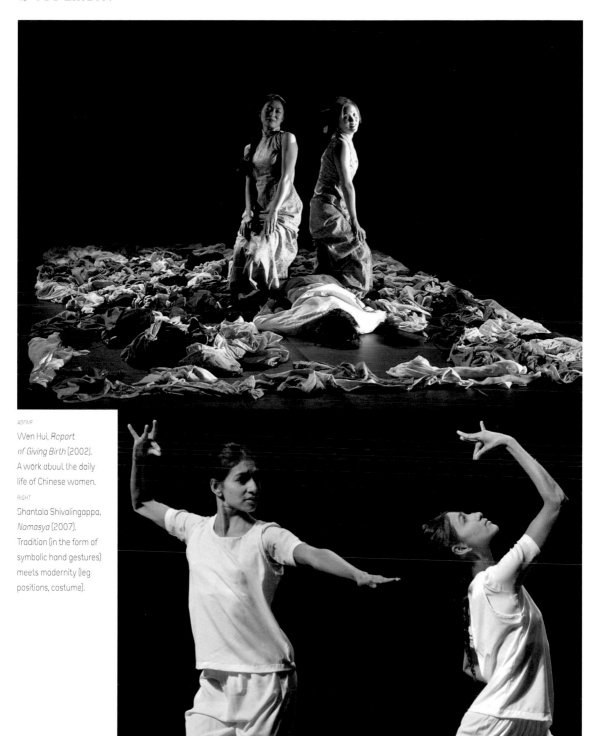

ABOVE
Wen Hui, *Report of Giving Birth* (2002). A work about the daily life of Chinese women.
RIGHT
Shantala Shivalingappa, *Namasya* (2007). Tradition (in the form of symbolic hand gestures) meets modernity (leg positions, costume).

Saburo Teshigawara, *Miroku* (2008).
The extreme precision of this solo requires the dancer-choreographer to occupy the theatrical space with flawless skill.

PAGE 124
Padmini Chettur, *Pushed* (2006).
Back-to-back like Siamese twins, the dancers
elaborate a spare yet highly refined performance.

PAGE 125
Ea Sola, *Sécheresse et pluie, volume 2* (Drought and Rain, 2005).
Revisiting the original work, Ea Sola explored
Vietnam's troubled memories.

BALLET TODAY

If you're nostalgic for toe shoes, arabesques, and exquisite pas de deux, then don't worry, we've found something to satisfy your legitimate craving, thanks to a generation of choreographers with occasionally classical training. In the twenty-first century it's now okay to look enthusiastically to the past and to dust off some old steps. Not only is not unfashionable, it's positively chic!

Obviously, the great heroines of classical ballet are practically immortal—the likes of Giselle, Sylvia, Manon, and Odette/Odile (not forgetting valiant princes and a few bashful lovers) still pack glamorous theaters such as the Paris Opera, Covent Garden, and the Marinsky and Bolshoi theaters, to mention just a few. Audiences never seem to tire of performances by ethereal ballerinas.

British choreographer Matthew Bourne has grasped the potential of these heroines, whom he has revived in his own manner. When Bourne brought *Swan Lake* out of the closet, the prince turned out to be gay, fantasizing over male swans in their irresistibly feathered shorts. (This was the ballet shown in the final scene of the film *Billy Elliot,* ending the story of a young English lad who dreamed of being a dancer rather than a soccer player.) Since then, Bourne has put a new shine on Carmen (*Car Man*) and *The Nutcracker.* His choreography simplifies gestures, somewhat like the subtext of a musical, so that every movement has meaning. Bourne's triumph with *Swan Lake* was a reassuring development for the future of ballet. Even bolder is Michael Clark, another jewel in the British crown who worked for the Royal Ballet before transforming himself into a bad boy and punk prince charming. Although not all his pieces are unforgettable, his Stravinsky triptych is a wonderful exercise in style in which the pas de deux flies at a breakneck speed, the lifts are heavenly, and the leaps are weapons of massive seduction. Drawing on a reservoir of dancers with obvious academic baggage, Clark has rewritten the history of ballet. Even if his princesses sometimes sport moustaches or leather, they always bear their heads as befits their rank.

A maverick choreographer on the French scene, Thierry Malandain, seems to waver between well-intentioned classical ballet and well-behaved modern dance. But it is worth taking the time to appreciate his work, which flaunts its classic skills yet is unhesitatingly challenging when flirting with Mozart and Ravel.

Clearly, then, updating classical ballet can turn a choreographer into a bona fide contemporary. Benjamin Millepied, a Frenchman with the New York City Ballet (where pioneering choreographers Balanchine and Robbins forged American neoclassical dance) knows this situation well. After early works that already attracted critical acclaim, Millepied produced a delightful *Nutcracker* for the Ballet du Grand Théâtre in Geneva; with the help of Paul Cox's sets, Millepied lightened the bravura passages in order to lend the magical tale the lightness of a snowflake. He struck again, in a more abstract vein, with *Amoveo* and *Triade* for the Paris Opera Ballet. The dance became more complicated, with a pas de trois in which the trio's legs "knitted together" as hips swayed. Meanwhile, the corporeal experimentation of Christopher Wheeldon, an Englishman who made his name in the United States, retains a classic feel—respect for traditional figures (couples, foursomes) and speed of execution—yet takes risks with modern scores and gliding floor work. Obviously, tiaras are out—and, sacrilegiously, there are fewer and fewer tutus—but you can still lift a leg or pull off a "six o'clock" (a spectacular position in which the legs are perfectly aligned, one on the ground, the other extending straight upward) without passing for an old fogey.

An American from San Francisco, Alonzo King, does just that: with his virtuoso vocabulary, he strips the stage of extraneous sets, alternates toe shoes with bare feet (for the ladies), and invites Shaolin monks to participate in a new production (*Long River High Sky,* 2007). He has brought color to today's ballet; in fact, as a black choreographer in an overly white world, King is a herald of change. The next hero of classical ballet may well hail from Mumbai or Johannesburg. **The next chapter remains to be written. Dance—Sleeping Beauty that she is—is just waiting for the eternal kiss.**

RIGHT

Benjamin Millepied, *Triade* (2008), Audric Bezard and Marie-Agnès Gillot with the Paris Opera Ballet in a tribute to Jerome Robbins.

FOLLOWING PAGES

Thierry Malandain, *Les Créatures* (2004). In a blend of genders, the director of the Ballet Biarritz dressed both men and women in wonderful black tutus.

PAGE 130

Michael Clark, *Mmm... Stravinsky Project, Part 2* (2008). The bad boy of English dance presented a series of ballets, often ironic, inspired by Stravinsky.

PAGE 131

Alonzo King, *Long River High Sky* (2008). This African-American choreographer, based in San Francisco, excels in astonishing trios.

TRADITIONAL DANCE FORMS

If you like to travel in time and space, then you'll enjoy dances often intended for traditional gods or spirits. Whether from India, Thailand, or Spain, they provide a refreshing vision. These traditional forms of dances are today being revisited by creative choreographers, lending them a contemporary touch.

Once known only to worldwide travelers or, occasionally, to cognoscenti, traditional forms of dance began to travel beyond their own borders in the twentieth century. But it was not until hard-to-categorize artists, often from the theater and dance worlds, took an interest in them that these parallel worlds were brought to public attention. Such artists include Maurice Béjart and Ariane Mnouchkine (France), Bob Wilson and Peter Sellars (the United States), and Peter Brook (halfway between Britain and France), all of whom actively built bridges. Guest invitations, exchanges, and contacts led to fusions. Nowadays, this approach is being perpetuated by younger artists such as Akram Khan (an Anglo-Bengali who as a boy notably worked on Brook's famous staging of the *Mahabharata*, the Sanskrit epic of Indian mythology, in a show that lasted nearly a whole day). Although now a well-known contemporary choreographer, Khan continues to practice kathak, a traditional form of classical dance from northwest India, combining both pure dance and narrative storylines, originally danced primarily by men. Kathak originated in the days of itinerant bards called *kathaks*, that is to say, storytellers. The dance is based on specific movements of both feet and hands, yet also features whirling pirouettes that terminate in statuesque poses. In his performances of kathak (*Polaroid Feet*, 2001, *Gnosis*, 2010), Khan adds modern color by dancing in simple shirt and trousers, dancing in profile (rather than frontally), and teasing his musicians. Nor did he balk at including this kathak (a dance both sacred and secular since its ancient origins) in *Sacred Monsters*, the piece he choreographed for prima ballerina Sylvie Guillem. It represents yet another way of looking far ahead. Other forms of classical Indian dance, such as kuchipudi and bharata natyam—both highly codified—also find themselves regularly performed on stage.

Another original approach has been taken by Thai dancer Pichet Klunchun, a virtuoso of the royal dance in his native land, called khon. Klunchun has boldly shared the stage with Jérôme Bel, who comes up with some of the most inventive ideas on the French scene. The upshot was *Pichet Klunchun and Myself*, in which the two protagonists take the floor in turn, explaining their approach and their work, allowing Klunchun not only to delight audiences with examples of khon dance, but to take umbrage at the nudity in Bel's work. Indeed, this tactic of convergence was designed to lead to an understanding of differences as well as similarities, demonstrating that you don't dance for a deity or a king in the same way you do for an "ordinary" audience. Above all, *Pichet Klunchun and Myself* offered a glimpse of two creative artists exploring their own doubts; and from such uncertainties there emerged a lesson in sharing.

It would be remiss to overlook flamenco, a traditional form of dance that some people dismiss as folk art. It was poorly viewed in the days of Franco's dictatorship, but in the early twenty-first century flamenco has been championed by new conquistadors by the names of Andrés Marin, Mercedes Ruiz, and Israel Galván. They have revived the fundamentals of flamenco before mixed audiences composed of long-time fans, purists, and fashionable young people, all of whom lap it up. Flamenco, an art of nomads whose origins apparently go back to India (whence gypsies originally set out on their migration toward Seville and Jerez de la Frontera), is in fact highly codified in terms of footwork (*zapateado*), wrist position, and hip movements. The art has had its hard times, and for a while was limited to tourist cabarets and *tablaos* (cafés where performers sing and dance). The likes of Marin and Ruiz do not totally renounce that period, but they exploit the movement and music—not forgetting the all-important poetry—to create striking gestures and blazing figures. Galván, currently one of the biggest stars of flamenco following the legendary Farruco, even dares to dance on stage with sophisticated set designs (a kind of ring, a moving platform). This trio of innovators—unlike that genius of flamenco Antonio Gadés, who underscored flamenco's theatrical aspect in *Carmen* and *Bodas de sangre* (Blood Wedding)—stick close to basic instincts. And to dance. You'll surely develop a taste for it.

FAR LEFT
Israel Galván,
Arena (2004).
Galván's mastery
dazzles as he performs
a toreador-like duet
with a rocking chair,
staged by Pedro G.
Romero.

LEFT
Akram Khan,
Polaroid Feet (2002).
Moving back and forth
between contemporary
dance and traditional
kathak, Khan takes his
audience on a trip to
sacred—and swinging—
India.

FOLLOWING PAGES
Israel Galván,
Arena (2009).
This dynamic solo,
featuring Galván in
his signature profile
stance, sparks
a dialogue with
flamenco artists
and a rock group.

They pop up in conversations, reviews, and articles. The key words of contemporary dance. These definitions aid navigation among choreographic concepts and propositions. This quick overview is designed to shed some light before—or after—a show. For readers who wish to explore further, there are now entire dictionaries of dance in English. Until you acquire one, however, you can enjoy testing yourself on the terms below.

ABSTRACTION

It might be said that abstraction discards models that derive from everyday reality alone. Abstraction does not try to depict what *is*, but rather explores a special idiom (or language) that does not involve imitating an expression or feeling. It is therefore is the exact opposite of mime and Romantic ballet. From Loïe Fuller to Merce Cunningham, not forgetting Alwin Nikolais, abstraction reflects, to a certain extent, the twentieth-century artistic trend that revolutionized painting, as epitomized by Wassily Kandinsky, Piet Mondrian, and Kazimir Malevich.

BUTOH

Invented in Japan in the 1950s, Butoh takes its name from the Japanese words for dance (*bu*) and stamp the ground (*toh*). Simultaneously rejecting Western classical and modern dance as well as Japan's own traditions of performing arts, Butoh sought to be a dance of the "dark body," influenced by Buddhism and Shintoism. This minimalist school employs few effects and few sets, instead celebrating the rites of passage of life with an economical body language; its dancers perform nearly naked, face and body covered in white, in a slow and magnificent ritual.

CONTACT

In dance, "contact" refers to the physical contact between the body and an exterior element on which it rests or is placed. The weight of the body thus encounters "resistance." Although feet-versus-ground is most common form of contact, it is not the only one—contact/improvisation technique has led to the exploration of body-versus-body contact.

FALLS

The action of falling on the dance mat (often repeatedly, since apparently no two falls are the same) functions as a counterpoint to the well-known technique—particularly in ballet—of upward extension into space. Many choreographers explored falls throughout the twentieth century, but there was a specific infatuation with them in the 1980s. Devilishly physical movements were favored by Flemish choreographers Anne Teresa De Keersmaeker and Wim Vandekeybus, who relentlessly fell, rolled, or collapsed. Such movements are still an essential hallmark of creative choreography today.

FREE DANCE

Largely stemming from the work of François Delsarte (an educator and theorist of movement), free dance was a major trend of the late nineteenth century that broke with the codes of so-called classical ballet. It involved a sensorial approach to movement via breathing, thrust, and awareness of weightiness. Free dance as explored by the likes of Loie Fuller, Ruth St. Denis, Isadora Duncan, and Alexander Sakharoff paved the way for many twentieth-century trends from modern dance to contemporary dance.

IMPROVISATION

In dance, improvisation refers to actions that have not been choreographed or worked out in advance. It is a dance of the present moment, as compared to a known, rehearsed movement. Improvisation could be seen in the work of pioneering dancer Isadora Duncan. Some American choreographers such as Anna Halprin and Trisha Brown practiced various kinds of improvisation (collective improvisation, for example). Steve Paxton developed contact/improvisation in which two partners start from a point of contact between their bodies and then execute a series of improvised movements. Finally, improvisation is also a part of certain traditional forms of dance such as flamenco.

LIFT

A lift involves a joint movement in which one dancer carries another. It can of course be extended to more than two performers and it covers a wide variety of moves. Lifts have been part of classical ballet since the nineteenth century and still survive in modern and contemporary dance. There is even a group lift, as seen in Maurice Béjart's *Rite of Spring* in which the Chosen One is literally raised up by the whole company.

MODERN DANCE

This term covers the dance trends that emerged in the United States in the early twentieth century, in opposition to classical dance technique. Martha Graham, Doris Humphrey, Jose Limon, and Alwin Nikolais were representatives of this trend. The role of Merce Cunningham is trickier—some historians locate him in the modern dance tradition while others place him in the postmodern trend. Modern dance preceded the postmodern dance of the 1970s.

NON-DANSE (NON-DANCE)

A term that emerged in France in the 1990s to describe the work of certain choreographers—often former dancers who first came to notice in the 1980s—who staged physical movement in a non-dance way, often involving extreme slowness, nudity, allusions to other arts, and performance. Such choreographers dared to present dance performances in which corporal virtuosity was not the only goal. Nevertheless, most of the choreographers in question (from Jérôme Bel to Boris Charmatz via Vera Mantero and Christian Rizzo) rejected this term, which is falling into disuse.

NOTATION

The act of "transcribing" movement through a system of writing. Various systems of notation have been used according to period ever since the fifteenth century. The great names associated with notation include Toulouze, Feuillet, and, more recently, Laban, Benesh, and Nikolais. Although certain choreographers such as Angelin Preljocaj still prefer written notation, video recordings have now become the prime way of archiving choreographic works.

NOUVELLE DANSE (NEW DANCE)

Refers to the trends that emerged in the late 1970s and early 1980s in certain European countries, led by France and including Belgium, Italy, Spain, and Great Britain as well as Canada on the other side of the Atlantic. In French, the term nouvelle danse was quickly replaced by "contemporary dance." Both terms cover creative choreographers from a variety of schools.

POINTE WORK

Dancing on the tip—or pointe—of the toes is known as "pointe work," done in the notorious pointe shoes (or toe shoes). Associated with the classical and neoclassical schools of ballet, pointe work can now be regularly seen in the work of certain contemporary choreographers such as Angelin Preljocaj, Jan Fabre, and Édouard Lock. William Forsythe employed pointe work in the 1980s to lend greater speed to his gestural idiom.

POSTMODERN DANCE

As distinct from American modern dance, postmodern dance emerged in the 1960s and 1970s. It rejected not so much the classical idiom or modern composition as the idea of virtuosity for virtuosity's sake, as well as expressionism. As a reflection on the body and its surrounding environment, postmodern dance drew inspiration from the visual arts, from performance art, and improvisation techniques; the best representatives of the movement, each in his or her own way, include Trisha Brown, Lucinda Childs, Steve Paxton, and Yvonne Rainer. The influence of this highly diverse trend is now widely acknowledged.

STAGING

In dance this term refers to the scenic space or environment in which the dancer performs. A stage director will work in collaboration with the choreographer to create the overall staging, which takes into account the sets, lighting, and sound. Stage design is becoming increasingly important in performances of contemporary dance, just as it is in the theater.

TANZTHEATER (DANCE THEATER)

Tanztheater first appeared in Germany in the 1920s as a choreographic concept that incorporated aspects of theater through the use of a certain expressiveness, including speech and dramatic effects. To a certain extent, Tanztheater is "heir" to German Expressionism. The movement's two most important advocates were Kurt Jooss, who founded the Folkwang Tanztheater Studio in Essen in the early twentieth century, followed by Pina Bausch in the 1970s.

TURN-IN

The act of turning the tips of the toes inward (in contrast to classical technique of turn-out). Perhaps the best example of this "technique" remains Vaslav Nijinsky in his famous Rite of Spring. More recently, performers of Japanese Butoh have adopted this position for the lower half of the body, with both knees and feet rotated inward.

DANIEL LARRIEU ✸ *Waterproof* (1986, revived 2006)

1913

THE RITE OF SPRING
BY VASLAV NIJINSKY

No one in the brand new Théâtre des Champs-Élysées in Paris on the evening of May 29, 1913, suspected the extent of the scandal about to occur: during the program of dance presented by Sergey Diaghilev's Ballets Russes, the audience—although accustomed to the company's bold initiatives—turned the première of *The Rite of Spring* into a verbal boxing match. Diaghilev, an early incarnation of a marketing maven, came up with what transpired to be the disastrous idea of hiring a claque to applaud with great vigor the new piece choreographed by the house protégé, Vaslav Nijinsky. But soon insults were being swapped between those for and those against *The Rite*. The indescribable pandemonium that followed prevented the dancers from following Igor Stravinsky's score, which was nevertheless being calmly conducted by Pierre Monteux. It is said that an enraged Nijinsky, standing on a chair in the wings, tried to mark the beat for his dancers as well as he could. His *Rite of Spring*, now considered a major twentieth-century ballet, would have only four performances in Paris and three in London before vanishing forever. In a supreme insult, Diaghilev himself commissioned a new version in 1920 from choreographer Léonide Massine.

The ballet's reception can be partly explained by the novelty of its music and its choreography. Stravinsky acknowledged that he had composed a score that "appeal[ed] neither to the spirit of fairy tales nor to human joy and grief but in which I strive toward a somewhat vaster abstraction." He furthermore realized he would "confuse those [people] who have until now manifested precious sympathy toward me." Nijinsky's choreography, meanwhile, was inspired by images of pagan Russia: the two-act *Rite of Spring* recounts the worship of Mother Earth followed by the sacrifice of a virgin known as the Chosen One. On stage, dancers executed steps with feet turned inward, underscoring the impression of figures ill at ease with their bodies. Many people in the audience saw only coarseness and folk art; and yet this ballet was nothing less than the harbinger of modernism in dance. And it would ultimately enjoy its own new spring once Robert Joffrey met Marie Rambert, who had danced in the première. After reading Rambert's notes, Joffrey decided to revive it. The real trigger, however, had been Millicent Hodson who, as a student writing her dissertation on the Ballets Russes, had spent years on an investigation worthy of a crime novel, tracking down original members of this choreographic odyssey and uncovering rare documents in order to retranscribe Nijinsky's original choreography as "faithfully" as possible. In 1987 the Joffrey Ballet triumphantly performed the revived *Rite of Spring* at the Théâtre des Champs-Élysées, and in 1991 this unique reconstitution entered the repertoire of the Paris Opera ballet company, where it still—rightly—remains.

1932

THE GREEN TABLE
BY KURT JOOSS

Kurt Jooss's masterpiece, *Der Grüne Tisch* (The Green Table), was not just an exemplary work of Tanztheater, it was also an act of rebellion. In the 1920s, Jooss had worked with the theorist and educator Rudolf Laban, all the while perfecting his skills by taking classical ballet classes. In 1927 he founded the Folkwang Hochschule in Essen, Germany, where he put these theories into practice. In 1929 the Laban and Jooss schools ultimately merged.

Jooss emphasized the theatrical aspect of dance, as perfectly illustrated by *The Green Table*. It is a ballet in eight tableaux, not unlike a danse macabre with striking masks and makeup. The story concerns the endless renewal of war due to the endlessness of negotiations that take place around a large table covered—of course—in green baize cloth. The figure of Death, who seems to manipulate all the other characters, winds up leading the dance and thereby leading men, in their folly, to their own deaths. The only character who escapes is the dealer. This narrative, expressionist ballet assumed a more political dimension with the rise of Nazism in Germany, dragging Europe toward the Second World War. *The Green Table* was nevertheless first performed at the Théâtre des Champs-Élysées in Paris as part of an international choreography competition held in memory of Jean Börlin. The contest was launched by the Archives Internationales de la Danse, run by Rolf de Maré, who had moreover founded the Ballets Suédois. After winning first prize, *The Green Table* was continually performed by Jooss's company—but not in his home country. He left Germany in 1934 when the Nazi government instructed him to fire his Jewish employees. Jooss refused and moved to London with his family, returning to Essen only fifteen years later, in 1949. There, his revamped school served as a crucible for new talents; his students included Pina Bausch, Susanne Linke, and Reinhild Hoffmann, all of whom, in a way, have perpetuated Jooss's lessons in courage as well as dance. Meanwhile, Jooss's own daughter, Anna Markand, supervised the adoption of *The Green Table* into the repertoires of companies the world over, such as the Joffrey Ballet and the American Ballet Theater. A torch was passed, and art was the victor.

1946

LE JEUNE HOMME ET LA MORT
(THE YOUNG MAN AND DEATH)

BY ROLAND PETIT
WITH JEAN BABILÉE

As a dancer and, above all, choreographer, Roland Petit holds what might be described as an uncomfortable place in the history of dance. Some commentators see him as a neoclassicist (he staged music-hall shows for his wife and muse, Zizi Jeanmaire, and attempted to launch a career in America), while others see him as a fixer whose greatest gift was his ability to recruit well-known writers, designers, and artists for his choreographic ventures: Jean Anouilh, Marcel Aymé, Yves Saint Laurent, David Hockney, and Max Ernst. Yet Petit was also—and especially—the man who choreographed *Carmen* (1949) and *La Dame de pique* (Queen of Spades, 1982). But they were surpassed by *Le jeune homme et la Mort*. Based on an idea by Jean Cocteau, this short piece is a romantic pas de deux between a young man and a young woman; he feverishly woos her with high hopes, while she insolently rejects him, going so far as to show him the rope with which he will hang himself.

Coming just after the Second World War, this ballet surprised people by its seriousness as well as its sense of spectacle. Wakhevitch's sets literally soared, offering a glimpse of Parisian rooftops and a reproduction of the Eiffel Tower blinking to the beat of a lighted sign advertising Citroën cars. That is where the Young Woman with death mask comes in, ultimately guiding her partner to a final, prodigious leap. The role of the Young Man was performed by the greatest French dancer of the day, Jean Babilée (partnered by Nathalie Philippart). During a famous

luncheon, Cocteau allegedly said to Babilée, "You're our Nijinsky, so I'll do you a 'modern' *Spectre de la rose*." Significantly, as a classical dancer, Babilée had never performed a role "without wig or doublet."

The studio rehearsals, directed by the choreographer Petit but under Cocteau's watchful eye, freed Babilée from the imperatives of classical ballet. The team tried out a number of "acrobatic movements and backward, slow-motion rolls" which were truly novel for the day and pointed toward the improvisations highly prized by contemporary dancers some twenty-five years later.

Another important detail concerned the costumes by Christian Bérard, who dressed Babilée in a notorious pair of overalls with one strap undone ("it came undone during rehearsals," recalled the dancer). Adding splatters of paint to the Young Man's costume was Cocteau's idea. Finally, although rehearsals were done to jazz and percussion beats, the music was only chosen later, using a method dear to Cocteau, called "accidental synchronization": the score was chosen on the basis of the running time of the choreography. Jean-Sebastian Bach's *Grand Passacaglia*, which lasted thirty-seven minutes, fit the bill. On the evening of the première, Babilée danced with a watch on his wrist to make sure he did not get ahead of the conductor, André Girard—it was not until the sixteenth minute that Babilée had to "hang himself" on stage.

And even if the set may seem a little outmoded nowadays, Petit's choreography has lost none of its modernity, having been largely ahead of its time. The greatest dancers, from Mikhail Baryshnikov to Nicolas Le Riche (star dancer with the Paris Opera Ballet), have performed this role of a lifetime—the lifetime of Jean Babilée.

1959

KINJIKI
(FORBIDDEN COLORS)

BY TATSUMI HIJIKATA

The eruption onto the Japanese scene in the 1950s of Butoh, a non-spectacular form of dance, could be described as an artistic earthquake, if an underground one. At that time, the performing arts were still dominated by traditional theatrical genres (from Noh to Kabuki, without forgetting the puppet theater known as Bunraku). But the emergence of a unique figure, Tatsumi Hijikata, would lead to a number of upheavals. Initially trained in modern dance, Hijikata had an open-minded attitude that lead him toward jazz, Spanish, and ballroom dance; and when he saw Kazuo Ohno on stage in 1949, it came as a revelation, for Ohno was dancing in an expressionist manner, having taken classes with a former student of Mary Wigman from Germany. The two men did not meet until 1954. And it was for Yoshito, Ohno's son, that in 1959 Hijikata choreographed *Kinjiki*, perhaps the founding work of the school of Butoh ("dance of darkness").

Kinjiki might be described not so much as a piece of dance as a performance. Hijikata scandalized people by drawing inspiration from Jean Genet (later he would stage versions of Lautréamont and Sade). Above all the highly sexed violence was anything but feigned—the boy, young Ohno, practically strangled a live chicken between his thighs, while Hijikata simulated a rape. But Butoh's still fledgling idiom was there for all to see: shaved skulls, nearly naked bodies dressed only in loincloth, and staccato (indeed, convulsive) movements. As a dancer and choreographer inspired by surrealism and critical of the modern society arising after the war, Hijikata made a big impression on peoples' minds. From one work to the next he sought a better grasp of "lessness," plumbed the depths of his inner self, sought to turn his flesh into "the repository of collective memory," and ultimately explored, in a return to roots, the everyday events of life in the 1920s in his home province of Tohoku.

Hijikata and his sidekicks Ohno and Akira Kasai were immediately accused of high treason toward "real," Westernized, dance. But they received the weighty approval of Japanese author Yukio Mishima. And young performers who took courses with students of Hijikata and Ohno perpetuated, in their own way, this tradition of inward-looking, soul-searching dance. Such was the case with the duo of Eiko and Koma, who now work in the United States, and Ushio Amagatsu, who would go on to found the Sakai Juku company, not to mention choreographer Carlotta Ikeda, who cofounded Ariadone in France with Ko Murobushi. Finally, in the 1980s, young Western dancers (such as Catherine Diverrès and Bernardo Montet)—strongly impressed by Kazuo Ohno's Western tours, notably with his solo *La Argentina*—began traveling to Japan on the trail of Butoh masters. In 2006, the terrific Japanese dancer Kim Itoh performed his own version of *Kinjiki* at the Biennale de la Danse in Lyon, France, as a distant tribute to the master, Hijikata. To a certain extent, things had come full circle, as Butoh entered the eternal sphere of dance.

1961
BOLÉRO
BY MAURICE BÉJART

It is not easy to choose just one date in Maurice Béjart's long, creative career that spanned over two hundred and fifty choreographic works. It would have been perfectly reasonable to opt for 1955, the year of *Symphonie pour un homme seul* (Symphony for a Lone Man), or 1959, the date of his version of *The Rite of Spring* (which remains, even today, one of Béjart's most frequently performed pieces). And yet, for various reasons, the 1961 première of *Boléro* appears to be the key date.

Béjart did not appear from out of nowhere when his work exploded on the French scene. His choreography rested on solid classical foundations, but he had managed to free movement through a dynamic inspired jointly by popular dance (from jazz to rock), by Martha Graham (that high priestess of dance), and by a certain theatricality. In the early 1960s Béjart's *Boléro* projected the image of a sovereign, adored body some years prior to the wave of sexual liberation. Duska Sifnios, who created the role in 1961, was followed at various times by Claude Bessy, Sylvie Guillem, and Marie-Agnès Gillot, all of whom left their mark on a brief but all-encompassing role that seems wedded to every line of Maurice Ravel's score. Such uninhibited ballerinas—we are indeed a long way from *Swan Lake*—incarnated Melody, soon to be surrounded by Rhythm, the male dancers who lurk nearby. The progression of movement around the raised stage steadily intensifies—like Ravel's music—up to the final delivery. To add to the nascent legend of this *Boléro*, Béjart had the bright idea of reversing the main role, which he alternately assigned to male dancers, thus making his *Boléro* the first work to go beyond genres. Its success continued unabated, permanently installing the young Béjart among the rare pantheon of the stars of modern dance. His notorious *Boléro*—or, at least, an excerpt—would even appear in a film by Claude Lelouch, *Dance of Life*. It was Jorge Donn, Béjart's favorite dancer, who absolutely incarnated the role—in the mind of the general public, the two would be forever linked even after their deaths, first that of Donn, then Béjart. *Boléro* is the modern yet popular ballet par excellence. The stuff of legend.

Maurice Béjart, *Boléro* (1961). Entranced by the rhythm,
Nicolas Le Riche, étoile with the Paris Opera Ballet, lets himself go until the ecstatic finale.

1969

THE BAGNOLET DANCE CONTEST

After the social upheavals of 1968, but for reasons that had more to do with politics and the state of society, creative dance enjoyed is own period of revolution. In 1969, a competition was organized by Jacques Chaurand in Bagnolet, on the outskirts of Paris; this annual event would constitute a key landmark on the horizon of contemporary dance in France. Initially dubbed Le Ballet pour Demain (Ballet for the Future), the contest was held in a suburban gym and, thanks to the imagination and flair of the former-dancer-cum-organizer, it was open to everything at first: jazz, classic, modern, and contemporary dance. The original spirit seems to have had less to do with competing than with sharing.

Later rechristened Le Concours de Bagnolet (Bagnolet Dance Contest), this forum for young choreographers and dancers consistently revealed emerging talents on the contemporary scene. The list of participants who later went down in history is impressive—Jean Pomarès, Dominique Bagouet, Karine Saporta, Susanne Linke, Maguy Marin, Reinhild Hoffmann, Dominique Boivin, François Verret, Jean-Claude Gallotta, Régine Chopinot, Joëlle Bouvier and Régis Obadia, Philippe Decouflé, Mark Tompkins, Mathilde Monnier, and Angelin Preljocaj. The Bagnolet Contest became a badge of success that often raised the profile and programming possibilities of the winners, although it ultimately became a victim of its own success, and by the early 1980s its influence had begun to wane. In 1980, in fact, a symposium on dance (Les Assises de la Danse) was instituted as a kind of extension of the contest—a dynamic art was demanding more serious recognition from institutions that still largely continued to ignore it. The year 1981 brought a new, socialist government to France that was responsive to such requests. And yet the Concours de Bagnolet had only a few years of life left in its original form, for it was rejected by the generation of the 1990s, which castigated the idea of competition and prizes. The event nevertheless allowed isolated creative choreographers to meet and exchange ideas (and sometimes dancers!). And it now reminds us that many of the leading names of the nouvelle danse had been active back in the mid-1970s: Dominique Bagouet presented Chansons de nuit (Night Songs) there in 1976 and Maguy Marin premiered Nieblas de niño (Fog of Childhood) in 1978

(although it was the 1981 May B. that made her name). Finally, the Bagnolet Contest did not lead to a ghettoization of the new movement—the serious approach of someone like Verret mixed well with the unchecked whimsy of a Decouflé, while the expressive movements of the likes of Linke could be seen alongside the feminist baroque of Saporta. It might even be said that the third choreographic millennium—although its history has yet to be written, of course—is not as open-minded as Bagnolet was. The name of Bagnolet may no longer mean much to younger generations, but the current festival known as the Rencontres Chorégraphiques Internationales in Seine-Saint-Denis is, in a way, its heir; the new event has no winners, but displays marked curiosity for dances that tell of the world with its artistic revolutions. More than a copy, it is a tribute.

1970

THE MUDRA SCHOOL OPENS

When Maurice Béjart opened a school called Mudra within the walls of his own company in Brussels, The Ballet of the 20th Century, people were unaware of the revolution it would trigger. As the son of a philosopher, Gaston Berger, Béjart probably acquired a taste for learning and teaching. He wanted his school to be free, and to target young dancers between the ages of sixteen and twenty, selected by audition. The curriculum included not just courses in classical and modern dance, obviously, but also—and above all—a range of other courses. Apprentice performers were thus able—obliged?—to learn traditional Indian dances, flamenco, yoga, mime, acting, the arts of the circus, and rhythm. The education was an opening onto the world and into oneself, which was a real novelty in the 1970s, just prior to the great upheaval in choreography. Perhaps the finest testimony comes from Maguy Marin, a classically trained dancer who decided to liberate herself after having met students from the National Theater in Strasbourg. "I had been dancing for ten years. And then I discovered that something else existed. But where could I go? I looked for schools and that's how I heard about Mudra, the multidisciplinary school that Maurice Béjart had opened in Brussels. I studied there for three years. That's where I discovered all the things that can open up a young mind, that's where I became not so much 'an adult' as 'autonomous.'" A dancer's personal development and sense of well-being derived from improvisation, game-playing, and music lessons rather than just long

Maguy Marin, May B. (1981). A leading figure on the new dance scene in France,
Maguy Marin studied at Béjart's school, Mudra, then won the annual dance contest at Bagnolet.

hours at the bar. Béjart realized that modern dancers needed to be multiple beings. The performances given at the school, novel for the times, set the tone. And Mudra also served as a recruiting ground for Béjart's own company, the Ballet of the 20th Century—the master did not hesitate to hire certain graduates such as Marin herself. Pierre Droulers, Michèle-Anne de Mey, and Anne Teresa De Keersmaeker from Belgium, like Hervé Robbe and Yann Le Gac from France, spent time at Mudra before launching careers as dancers and choreographers. The extraordinary saga of Mudra lasted until 1987, and produced a shorter-lived African branch, Mudra-Dakar (1977–80). Many of Béjart's detractors are nevertheless thankful for his unique school that, in its way, contributed to the development of contemporary dance in Europe. Its very name meant a great deal to a man of many cultures like Béjart: mudras are the special positions of the hands associated with the main poses of the Buddha. Enlightenment can set you dancing.

feet in fresh peat, the Chosen One readied herself for sacrifice in a muddied gown. The vision that Bausch placed before audiences was sufficiently unsettling to increase local hostility to the new Tanztheater. A piece like *Barbe-Bleue* (Bluebeard, 1977), with excerpts from Béla Bartók's music that seemed to career across a gramophone, further alienated people. In short, it was the recognition that came from abroad, via festivals in places like Nancy, France, and successful appearances in Paris, that changed things. Different, more open, audiences discovered this dance theater where performers spoke on stage, where they paraded around in long gowns and suits to replay games of love, chance, and cruelty. Wuppertal, the city of Bayer factories and a famous overhead tram, "The Suspension Line" (as seen in Wim Wenders's film *Alice in the Cities*), finally found itself on the map—of international choreography. And now Wuppertal, which saw its muse pass away in the summer of 2009, will be forever grateful to Pina Bausch.

1973

PINA BAUSCH
BECOMES DIRECTOR OF THE
WUPPERTAL OPERA BALLET

In 1973 Pina Bausch, who as a young girl was sad to have a "rubber body" and who trained at the school in Essen prior to a solo career in the United States, was offered the post of director of dance at the Wuppertal Opera. Bausch was totally unaware of the public's reservations and its attachment to the traditional company. With regard to her first few months there, Bausch referred to "a huge misunderstanding—the audiences thought my work was a provocation, but it wasn't!" She also had to convince the resident dancers to learn a new repertoire and to acquire a new gestural idiom—which led most of the classically trained dancers to leave the company. Another task of reconstruction faced Bausch, who in certain interviews mentions her fear at those moments. "I would lose confidence but I felt strong enough to avoid ever making compromises." At the start she nevertheless relied on composers known to the public, such as Gluck for *Iphigénie en Tauride* and *Orphée et Eurydice* and Mahler for *Fritz* and *Adagio: Fünf Lieder von Gustav Mahler*.

In 1975 Bausch choreographed her own very personal version of Stravinsky's *Rite of Spring*. The dancers had their

1975

MIKHAIL BARYSHNIKOV
DANCES IN
JOHN BUTLER'S *MEDEA*

In order to appreciate the significance of this performance by a star of classic ballet, it is obviously important to establish both work and performer in their contexts. Baryshnikov, a prodigal dancer who trained in Riga before joining the Kirov Ballet in Leningrad (now Saint Petersburg), defected to the West during a 1974 tour of Canada—another clash in ballet's cold war. Misha, as Mikhail is known, joined the American Ballet Theater immediately after his defection; he was a classical dancer par excellence despite his relatively small stature. For American audiences he was the perfect prince, a combination of technical virtuosity and grace. In the 1970s he became the public face of dance, as well as a star in the United States, where he appeared in films like *The Turning Point* (1980) and *Dancers* (1987). But the "revolution" that Baryshnikov brought to the still-closed world of classical ballet lay elsewhere (an open mind is in fact his main character trait). In 1975, he created the role of Jason in *Medea* by John Butler, a choreographer who had danced with Martha Graham and who invented a style that borrowed from classicism but lent it modern color. There where other stars would have taken

Pina Bausch, *Sweet Mamba* (2008). Long flowing gowns for the ladies, dark suits for the gentlemen (usually designed by Marion Cito): Bausch's costumes were part of her legend.

to their heels, Baryshnikov eagerly learned the new role (with ballerina Carla Fracci as his partner). It opened the door to other, increasingly demanding, collaborations: Twyla Tharp's *Push Comes to Shove* and Alvin Ailey's *Pas de Duke* the following year. Having suffered a knee injury in 1982, Baryshnikov began a new career by founding, with choreographer Mark Morris, the White Oak Dance Project, whose finest production was a program that paid tribute to Judson Church, titled *Past Forward*, with pieces by Steve Paxton, Trisha Brown, Yvonne Rainer, Simone Forti, David Gordon, and Deborah Hay. Audiences came to see the superstar Baryshnikov and discovered a whole historic realm of American postmodern art. This unusual venture transformed Baryshnikov into a model for many contemporary dancers and choreographers and thus places him outside the current classical–modern divide.

In 2005 he opened the Baryshnikov Arts Center in New York, designed to present or simply help cutting-edge artists. And in 2008 the sixty-year-old dancer was a dazzling partner to Anna Laguna in *The Place*, a duet by Swedish choreographer Mats Ek. That same year, Baryshnikov told this author that he had no idea what he would be doing the following year. "I've always tried to keep some spontaneity. Let's just say that I have less time in my life to dance. And so much to live for." A true lesson in humility.

1980

MAISON DE LA DANSE
OPENS IN LYON

A quiet revolution in dance occurred in Lyon, France, when a team of enthusiasts led by the visionary Guy Darmet decided to open a venue devoted solely to dance, La Maison de la Danse, in the Croix-Rousse neighborhood of the city. Thus in the month of June of that year, a program to herald the future opening of these symbolic premises featured the Lyon Opera Ballet, which premiered three new works: *Dumbarton Oaks* by Daniel Ambasch, *Contrastes* by Maguy Marin, and *Pile ou face* (Heads or Tails) by Quentin Roullier. The first full season, 1980–81, included works by some of the leading names in the new realm of movement, such as *Mouvements* by Jean-Claude Gallotta/Groupe Émile Dubois, *Le pré est vénéneux mais joli en automne* (The Meadow is Harmful but Pretty in the Fall) by Marie Zighera, *Apparences* by Claude Decaillot, *Les Portes d'Italie* (The Gates of Italy) by François Verret, the

Théâtre du Silence's *Pas et par* by David Gordon, *En partant de...* (Starting From...) by Brigitte Lefèvre, and *Pas de onze* (Elevenet) by Jacques Garnier.

The Maison de la Danse is still unique in France, although another has since been founded in Stockholm, Sweden. Which is not many. Thanks to political, artistic, and public support, Lyon's "house of dance" was able to move into the Théâtre du Huitième in September 1992, allowing it to maintaining a higher cruising speed with more subscribers and more invited companies.

In 1984, Darmet took on another task by becoming the artistic director of Lyon's newly launched Biennale Internationale de Danse, closely linked to the Maison de la Danse, as might be expected. The biannual autumn event went worldwide through a shrewd choice of special themes ranging from German dance to American dance via "The Silk Route" and, in 2008, "Retour en avant" (Return to the Future), which focused on the transmission of tradition through the revival or reinterpretation of key works (such as Carolyn Carlson's *Blue Lady* and Dominique Bagouet's *Petites pièces de Berlin*). Lyon's biennial of dance is aimed at the general public, and includes a parade of dancers through the streets of the city. It has no equivalent in Europe, although just outside Paris the Biennale du Val-de-Marne was launched in 1981 by Michel Caserta with more modest resources, on the heels of a dance festival held there in 1979; the biennial follows the development of contemporary dance in France all the while establishing bridges with the United States and Africa.

France is not only a land of dance but also a country of dance festivals. The pioneering event, no longer extant, was Danse à Aix, whose first edition in the summer of 1977 brought together Carolyn Carlson, Larrio Ekson, the Ballets de Nancy, the Ballet-Théâtre Joseph Russillo, and two star dancers from the Paris Opera, Jacqueline Rayet and Jean-Pierre Francetti, who performed Maurice Béjart's *Webern Opus 5*, not to mention a still-young prodigy, Dominique Bagouet, who danced *Suite pour violes* (Suite for Viols).

It was this same Bagouet, a key figure on the French contemporary dance scene, who launched the Montpellier dance festival in 1981, joined a few months later by Jean-Paul Montanari. The thirtieth edition of this festival was celebrated in 2010. Other French cities that organized festivals included Arles (no longer operational), Uzès, and Marseille, establishing a national network that was reinforced by the progressive opening of regional dance schools known as Centres Chorégraphiques. In 2008, the Théâtre National de Chaillot in Paris, once home to the likes of famous

Jean-Claude Gallotta, *Cher Ulysse* (Dear Ulysses, 2007).
This pas de deux between a dancer and a skeleton is a dynamic, danced version of a *vanitas* still-life.

theater directors Jean Vilar and Antoine Vitez, became a dance venue run by two choreographers, Dominique Hervieu and José Montalvo. France and dance, a natural rhyme.

1985
RÉGINE CHOPINOT HANGS DANCERS FROM ROPES

An icon of the new wave of choreographers, Régine Chopinot had already produced a dozen works when she undertook a groundbreaking project, *Rossignol* (Nightingale) in 1985. Chopinot, born in Algeria but based in La Rochelle, France, was young woman in a hurry, and she came to attention thanks to her energetic gestural idiom and her high-profile friends (designer Jean-Paul Gaultier, musician Ramuncho Matta, and her star performers such as Philippe Decouflé, Daniel Larrieu, and her own sister, Michèle Prélonge). With just a few pieces, from *Halley's Comet* to *Délices à Via*, Chopinot rose to the top. In the spring of 1985, in the city of Angers, she attempted the impossible: hanging her dancers from ropes. (Due to French theatrical superstition, the word "rope" [*corde*] was never uttered on stage, instead they referred to "threads.") The looked like strange marionettes on strings. Her largely young company included a Dutchman who had been to Béjart's Mudra school, Herman Diephuis, who recalled the new freedom the dancers discovered by being "wired." "It sparked our imaginations when we realized that dance could be something other than a leap in the air." Indeed, during *Rossignol,* the dancers spent a lot of time getting high. In a set composed of scaffolding, everyone flew around.

A few years later, Diephuis choreographed his first solo, titled *Trio à cordes*, which means String—or "Rope"—Trio. Tradition obviously dies hard. And yet there are good reasons why Chopinot might want to forget *Rossignol:* when it was revived in Paris, the technical crew realized that the Théâtre de la Ville, which was coproducing the show, was unsuited to the piece; so the production moved across town to the chic Théâtre des Champs-Élysées, which was still going strong ever since it had hosted the opening night of *The Rite of Spring.* But in January 1996 everything went wrong with *Rossignol:* the audience sitting along the sides of the second balcony could only see half the show. People began to yell and stamp their feet, and some even shouted, "We want our money back!" Rosella Hightower, a former star ballerina who had founded her own dance school, retorted, "Move lower!" Fisticuffs broke out in certain rows. (Herman Diephuis, meanwhile, witnessed yet another pitched battle in the history of contemporary dance when Jérôme Bel produced *The Show Must Go On* at the Théâtre de la Ville.) But Chopinot's *Rossignol* deserved better than this whiff of scandal—the choreographer, a daughter of the sea, wanted to play at flying, but nearly singed her own wings. Since those turbulent days, however, we know that it takes more to stop Chopinot.

1986
DANIEL LARRIEU PRESENTS WATERPROOF, AN AQUATIC BALLET

Water, water, everywhere! And dance, too. As incongruous as it may seem, dance and a pool full of water joined forces to yield *Waterproof*, a legendary work by Daniel Larrieu. People were already familiar with underwater ballets, of course; from the hallowed days of Esther Williams and her enchanted films in which the bathing beauty seems to float above and below Hollywood's artificial waves. But they primarily involved synchronized swimming as now practiced in the context of competitions.

Larrieu's idea was different. This endearing contemporary choreographer of the 1980s, working with the Centre National de Danse Contemporaine in Angers, reflected on the underwater roots of the body's gestural language. Right from the start, the venue itself—an indoor pool in Angers—was part of the show. A row of performers in a beam of light get straight to the heart of the matter—that is to say, into the water—as the hazy charm of an unreal dance begins to take effect. Beyond the mirror effect of reflections on water, work on the liquid surface produced elusive images of elongated bodies and quartered limbs. Walking with a featherweight cloak on the shoulders became a parade in a vacuum. Long hours of rehearsal were required for the ten dancers to move with such grace—Larrieu was concerned not so much with physical effort as with physical release. He didn't shirk from murkiness: *Waterproof* looked like a shadow ballet, from its magisterial opening (to the strains of Wagner's *Lohengrin*) to its watery round dance. In 2006, Larrieu and part of his team revived *Waterproof* in an anniversary

Daniel Larrieu, *Waterproof* (1986, revived 2006).
An intensely poetic, aquatic ballet, *Waterproof* played on effects of water that distorted—and magnified—movement.

version that retained the original, poetic feel. The now-legendary work resurfaced as choreography amid the waters: indeed, two screens showed the inside story, revealing legs at work beneath the water and replaying clips from the first version of *Waterproof* that included a (coincidental?) nod in the direction of the original sponsor, a watch manufacturer. It goes without saying that Larrieu was holding his breath during this slow-motion piece. Dance after dance, he raises questions about future directions—like the perpetual ripples that follows a solitary dive. The work is not only *Waterproof*, it has also become timeproof.

1992
PHILIPPE DECOUFLÉ STAGES
THE WINTER OLYMPIC GAMES

In 1992 the French city of Albertville organized the Winter Olympic Games. It charged contemporary choreographer Philippe Decouflé, practically unknown to the general public, with choreographing the opening ceremony. A worldwide TV viewing audience thus thrilled to Decouflé's three-dimensional poetry in motion. Decouflé was one of the young upstarts on the French dance scene, and he had considered careers in graphic novels, the circus, and mime before settling on dance. He came to the attention of that master of shapes and colors, Alwin Nikolais, who was teaching at the Centre National de la Danse Contemporaine in Angers. A supple dancer and a richly imaginative choreographer, Decouflé's early works with his company DCA—such as *Codex*—amazed people. Jean-Paul Goude, a designer with a flair for discovering new talent, recruited Decouflé for the huge parade to celebrate the bicentenary of the French Revolution in 1989; one of Decouflé's "tableaus," a clog dance, scored a hit. A long way from the dramatic theatricals favored by a stage director like Jérôme Savary, Decouflé's new form of "French show" hinged on the new trend of contemporary dance.

The challenge of the opening and closing ceremonies for the Olympic Games was nevertheless another thing altogether, involving an exceptional budget and a cast of hundreds of athletes, dancers, and extras in a venue—an Olympic stadium—that was light years from the cushy comfort of a theater. Furthermore, Decouflé had to conceive the piece for television, which would broadcast it live to the entire world. Following his 1990 ballet *Triton*, Decouflé spent two full years on the Olympic project. He recruited his "assistants," namely future choreographers such as Jérôme Bel and Herman Diephuis, and his favorite actor, Christophe Salengro (who would be the one-man-band of the event), and his wild costume designer, Philippe Guillotel (who was a crucial cog in the success of this large-scale artistic machine). On the night of the opening ceremony, the audience discovered a whimsical world of graceful skaters, ephemeral acrobats, fellows in snowflake suits, and a giant mobile from which hung crazy musicians with their drums. Decouflé celebrated the winter games and the nations with a sharp sense of staging, unlike most years when people watched a soulless spectacle. The constant inventiveness and ideas were designed to serve a message. It was probably the first time that an artist from the specialist field of contemporary dance was thus put in the spotlight: Decouflé appeared on the cover of weekly magazines, was interviewed on television, and was invited everywhere. The expression "contemporary choreographer" made its way into TV-speak. People don't really remember who won medals in 1992, but everyone recalls the grandiose opening ceremony.

Subsequently Decouflé, whose ballets had already attained a certain popularity, was offered a fortune to stage everything and anything. He produced a musical in Japan, but lost the bid for a revue for the Folies Bergère and for the Soccer World Cup in Germany. He did, however, meet the people running the Cirque du Soleil. "What I insist on is my ability to take in an interest in everything that relates to a show," he later commented. In 1994, two years after the impact of his Olympic Games, Decouflé presented *Petites pièces montées* (Little Ornamental Pieces), a kind of tribute to stagecraft, proving to all that he remained a lad who still marvels at the art of dance.

1993
MARIA LA RIBOT SELLS
HER *PIEZAS DISTINGUIDAS*

"A presentation rather than a performance," warned Maria José Ribot (known as La Ribot). It was just another way of maintaining her privacy—both personal and artistic—by measuring the exact distance between object-body and fantasy-body. The Spanish choreographer did not spring from just anywhere: her father was an art collector and her first husband was a painter. Above all, she studied both classical and

Philippe Decouflé, Opening Ceremony, Winter Olympic Games, Albertville (1992).
Not just a suitable tribute to winter sports, Decouflé's spectacular ceremony was a riot of fantastic imagery.

contemporary dance, although today she seems to take mischievous pleasure in ridding herself of these hampering influences. After founding her first company, Bocanada Danza, in tandem with Blanca Calvo in the 1980s, La Ribot committed herself entirely to *Piezas distinguidas* (Distinguished Pieces), a title that suggests a good deal about this unlikely Dada queen's (good) intentions.

These short pieces—halfway between *tableaux vivants* and unformatted performances—reflect a new economy: they were put up for sale. It was up to the lucky owner, initially a friend or relative, to contribute to a modest cycle of dances masterfully managed by the choreographer. It seemed an obvious approach for La Ribot, who said she didn't find it healthy to elaborate an entire structure before she even had a single idea. The hell with discourse: she pursued the creative process with *Mas distinguidas* and capped it with *Still Distinguished,* totaling several dozen short pieces in all. At first sight, she puts her body—usually nude—into play, sometimes using a prop such as a Polaroid camera that, once triggered, redraws the geography of the dancer's flesh. Or else she uses a folding chair that she mistreats, like a romantic partner on the edge of shared pleasure. But beyond these figures (of style), La Ribot is keenly interested in a more universal experience: "Even if it's very visual, I'm concerned above all with sexuality, as a living woman." La Ribot can be conjugated in the plural, an obvious fact that can be seen on stages that lack the imposed frontality of a theater. By simultaneously questioning the (show-biz) economy and the (art) market, she places artists at the center of her concerns. Her videos, as an extension of *Piezas distinguidas*, are now in the collections of museums in Spain and France. Finally, La Ribot has collaborated with other choreographers on certain projects such as *Gustavia* with Mathilde Monnier. One of her recent shows was titled *Illamame Mariachi,* while awaiting, perhaps, a traveling museum to come along for her *Piezas distinguidas.*

subjects such as homosexuality and the stereotyping of bodies by a society of superficial appearance that rejects differentness. Newson also dealt with "different" bodies in works such as *Can We Afford the Cost/The Cost of Living* (2000) followed by a second, more obvious version simply titled *The Cost of Living* (2003). He took his theory to its logical limits by casting a remarkable—but legless—dancer, David Toole. At the time Newson discussed *The Cost of Living* as a piece about people "who don't fit into the usual categories." So much of dance was about youthful, beautiful, and slender bodies—"a bit like a beauty contest." So he became hooked on this idea and composed his own vision of a contest on the artificial grass of the stage. In addition to Toole, an extraordinary performer, the company included a very fat dancer, which is equally rare. But Newson was not adapting *Freaks* to dance, he was trying to stimulate the audience's gaze, forcing it to ask questions—including educated audiences, which are maybe more stultified than they think. Somewhat provocatively, Newson refers to "Prozac faces," calling dance "the Prozac of the art forms. So that is what the piece is about—it's about those who aren't perfect and who can't pretend, those who don't fit in because they don't play the game." That is to say, the countless others that dance leaves by the wayside. The minority of minorities. But where is movement in all that, the reader may ask? That is probably Newson's great strength: he answers not through long speeches but through inventive body movements, as Toole notably demonstrated. In constant duets Toole manages to make us forget not his handicap, but our own—that is to say our way of seeing as different someone who is not quite like us. And when Toole is alone, walking on his hands, he is still—once again—dancing.

2004

LUC PETTON

MAKES BIRDS DANCE

Over the years we've seen various animals on stage (a dog, a horse) but never birds! Amateur ornithologist and choreographer Luc Petton pioneered this path with his "aviary" in 2004. Already noticed at the start of his career in the late 1990s for *Oscar,* a show in tribute to Oskar Schlemmer, the Bauhaus artist who composed *Triadic Ballet,* Petton launched another unique saga by combining birds and people on stage. His projected triptych carried

2003

LLOYD NEWSON DIRECTS

THE LEGLESS DANCER
DAVID TOOLE

Lloyd Newson is an unusual choreographer on the English scene, simultaneously social activist and a skilled company director. Right from the start in the 1980s, he dealt with hot

Luc Petton, *La Confidence des oiseaux* (The Confidence of Birds, 2008), Marie-Laure Agrapat.
A ballet truly for the birds—and dancers. Petton's next work is expected to combine the elements of air and water.

the evocative title of *La Confidence des oiseaux* (The Confidence of Birds), and came in two versions, one for indoor venues and another in the open air. On stage is a quartet of performers, in the wings are two bird handlers and an original "collection" of crows, jays, crimson rosellas (parrots), and magpies. The scenes that are danced, strictly speaking, are brief, since a bird cannot deal with more than ten minutes of "showtime." And certain species do not mix—which means that the preparation time for *La Confidence des oiseaux* is especially long. Not to mention complicated: the weight of these pretty pets must be monitored, not forgetting their reaction on stage. But the effort is worth it. The dancers in camouflage makeup and shorts, wearing a kind of fine wooden harness of their backs, seem to strike up a romantic display with the birds. Small wooden objects set on the stage and a mobile in the form of a perch also provide places for them to alight. The choreographic idiom is both simple—supple arabesques—and harmonious. In an exercise of rare poetic impact, one female dancer slowly unfolds her arms as a bird seems to run from the tip of one limb to the other. A soundtrack composed of sounds and music from nature accompanies this refreshingly artistic passage. Later, in a fuller gesture, the same dancer seems to toss the animal in the air: it unfolds its wings and quickly returns to her, in an inevitable nod to the "weightiness" of the dancers themselves. Here, Icarus is never far from the mind.

2009

MERCE CUNNINGHAM
CHOREOGRAPHS *NEARLY NINETY*

A symbol of American modernity—and beyond—all by himself, Merce Cunningham premiered an ambitious new ballet on April 16, 2009, the day of his ninetieth birthday. Not without irony, the new work was titled *Nearly Ninety*. On the stage of the venerable yet cutting-edge Brooklyn Academy of Music (BAM), *Nearly Ninety* proved once again that the master of contemporary dance still bubbled with ideas. In an almost futurist—and occasionally somewhat cumbersome—set by architect Benedetta Tagliabue with video design by Franc Aleu, *Nearly Ninety* teemed with pas de deux and trios that constantly invented new forms of dance.

In this "space of spaces" created by a mobile, folding structure, Cunningham once again invited other artists to collaborate with him; his faithful fellow traveler, musician Takehisa Kosugi, was joined by the legendary bassist John Paul Jones (formerly with Led Zeppelin) and the rock group Sonic Youth. The only rule was that the choreographic and musical compositions would take place separately. The dancers worked alone and did not discover the score until the curtain went up—or almost. Cunningham had previously established, when working with John Cage, this strict "separation of powers." The only unity was the performance time. On the day of *Nearly Ninety*'s final performance at BAM, all the former members of the Merce Cunningham Dance Company were hailed by the audience.

Just a few weeks after this triumph, Cunningham announced that he had made arrangements for the future. Given the "Martha Graham affair"—on her death, rights to her repertoire were disputed between her heir and the Graham Foundation and her dancers—the physically diminished Cunningham decided that after his death the company he founded would go on a two-year farewell tour, and would then be disbanded. His works, bequeathed to a foundation, could be performed by certain dance establishments according to specific rules. For each piece, a dance capsule containing video and working and staging documents would provide guidance as to the spirit of the choreography. Aware of the ephemeral nature of movement, Cunningham stated that, "It's really a concern about how you preserve the elements of an art which is really evanescent, which is really like water." Finally, bowing out with a handsome gift to his audience, Cunningham stipulated that the final performances in his adopted city of New York—which had the bright idea of declaring a Merce Cunningham Day—should have a single ticket price of ten dollars. Once an innovator, always an innovator. Merce Cunningham died on July 26, 2009. He is sorely missed.

Merce Cunningham, *Nearly Ninety* (2009), Merce Cunningham Dance Company.
Cunningham's final piece of choreography employed a mobile set, a structure that inevitably points to the future.

WILLIAM FORSYTHE ✳ *Artifact Suite* (2007). Ballets de Monte-Carlo

THEY DARED TO DO IT

bringing chance to dance:
MERCE CUNNINGHAM

A prodigious dancer known notably for his leaps, Merce Cunningham catapulted from modern dance as conceived by Martha Graham (with whom he danced until 1945) into his own universe. In addition to his formal emphasis on the line of the spinal column, Cunningham rejected narrative and psychological considerations. After a manifesto-like series of six solos to a score by John Cage in 1944, the choreographer struck another major blow in 1951 by introducing chance and randomness—elements totally alien to dance up till then—into *Sixteen Dances for Soloist and Company of Three*.

The principle was almost childish: combinations of movements were decided by tossing a coin. The ballet thus became a playground of unlimited possibilities where the dance sequences depended on a chance flip—of the coin! Cunningham's chance applied not only to sections and performers, but also to choreographic phrases, to the music, and to the set. Which meant that for the company, including Merce himself, the physical demands were matched by the need to memorize choreographic passages that were never the same from one performance to another.

Cunningham refined his concept of randomness with his first *Event* in 1964, which he composed from fragments of various works, a little like changing from one TV channel to another. The music was played by three musicians who each produced a special sound, some of which were "prepared sounds," others not. Cunningham always waited until he knew the venue before composing the structure for a given evening, so that two *Events* would never be alike. And he drew upon an enlarged repertoire—his own—to find the steps and gestures for *Events* that took place in museums, garden, or terrace.

In 1996, Cunningham, who since the beginning of that decade had been working with a computer program that allowed him to try out new combinations, boldly presented a work called *Rondo*. "Rolling the dice," stated Cunningham, "gives a moment of wonder, the imagination conjuring. A split second later, the dice at rest, the mind becomes active. Take a chance!"

More recently, with *eyeSpace* (2006), it was up to each member of the audience to play with chance, this time in terms of music, thanks to iPods supplied at the door. Each individual could reappropriate the work—notably including Mikel Rouse's score—by selecting the order of the pieces on the MP3 device. The aleatory become art with a capital A.

Although historians of dance recognize that chance has remained a marginal factor, since Cunningham is the only choreographer who took these ideas very far (as did, later, members of the Grand Union group)—it is impossible not to feel that the very spirit of this free approach, in the tradition of Stéphane Mallarmé and Marcel Duchamp, has influenced generations of dancers and choreographers. By no longer being chained to a narrative or musical framework, by employing abstraction to render the syntax of movement independent, contemporary dance entered a field of limitless potential—where, to a certain extent, it remains today.

Merce Cunningham, *eyeSpace* (2006), Merce Cunningham Dance Company. One-piece academic leotards, an exquisitely light group—Cunningham was notably inspired by birds.

dancing on raw earth:
PINA BAUSCH

When Pina Bausch, appointed director of the Wuppertal Opera Ballet two years earlier, presented her version of *The Rite of Spring* (with sets and costumes by Rolf Borzik) in December 1975, the ground seemed to have been well prepared. After all, even though the music by Stravinsky and choreography by Nijinsky had created a scandal at the Théâtre des Champs-Élysées when first produced, the work had since become a modern classic. Choreographers such as Mary Wigman and Maurice Béjart had already presented their interpretations of it. The storyline, drawn from Slavic folklore and pagan tradition, involved the sacrifice of a Chosen One, selected from among the group of participants. Stravinsky even referred to it as an "ancient Russian ceremony."

Bausch envisaged a powerful dance with women dressed in slips and men in dark trousers. Above all, she re-centered the action on the sacrificial Chosen One. But the real shock was the dance surface of the stage, which was covered with fresh, peaty earth that dirtied the bodies and faces of the dancers. Treading on this "soft" stage and maintaining balance was also a tiring exercise for the dancers. Years later Bausch stated that it was never her intention to make the performance "more difficult, but to make [the dancers] more aware of reality. I like reality. Life is never like a dance floor, smooth and reassuring."

Bausch, an iconic choreographer of the 1980s, also knew that certain works required a more conventional dance mat or stage surface. But whenever she had the chance, she and her associate (first Borzik, then Peter Pabst) would come up with strikingly original sets, such as the field of carnations for *Nelken* (Carnations, 1982) and the wall of bricks that collapses in *Palermo Palermo* (1989). Similarly, in recent years performers danced on water at the Wuppertal Tanztheater. "I like the experience of nature in relationship to dance. A dancer's foot falls completely differently on grass or soft earth, which means that his way of moving and being is completely changed," explained Bausch.* Her *Rite of Spring* has now entered the repertoire of the Paris Opera Ballet, earth included! In Bausch's wake, other choreographers explored landscapes of earth and other materials, but without matching her total success.

In treading soft ground, Bausch pointed the way toward other stage experiments that resonated with her dance,

simultaneously personal and open to the world around her. The stage, newly anchored in reality, became a pedestal for movement. In her last works, when Bausch used—some people felt she "abused"—water, she was returning to her roots, nothing more. Since that time there have been numerous sets and stagings that are unstable or shifting, not so much in a spirit of tribute as of experimentation. Exploring the gesture of falling—a reliable feature of 1980s dance—choreographers accompanied, so to speak, this movement with cluttered floors or mats that inflated or carpets you could crawl under. A new breath of life was catching up with dance—as Bausch precociously stated, life in no way resembles a smooth, slick dance mat. In her view—subsequently shared by many choreographers—the stage became a playground. With all its obstacles and setbacks. Welcome to the real world.

Pina Bausch, *The Rite of Spring* (1975).
Bausch's version of this key twentieth-century work earned the rare privilege of entering the repertoire of the Paris Opera Ballet in 1997.

*Pina Bausch, *Mot pour mot*, interview with Philippe Noisette (Van Dieren Éditeur, 1997).

distorting the body in *noumenon:*
ALVIN NIKOLAIS

The choreographer who once claimed he sought "motion, not emotion," was an artistic forerunner in a number of ways. The American-born Alwin Nikolais came from a mixed background—he had both Russian and German roots—and had been a practicing painter and a musician in his youth. But his attendance at a recital by dance pioneer Mary Wigman came as a revelation. He trained under one of her disciples, Truda Kaschmann, and also learned to handle marionettes, then opened his own school of dance. Nikolais presented an early, politically committed piece, *Eight Column Line*, before reality caught up with the budding choreographer: he was drafted into the army in the 1940s and fought in Europe.

On returning home, Nikolais was bursting with ideas ranging from the notation of movement (choroscript) to teaching dance to young children. But above all, Nikolais was an inventor of new forms. When he premiered *Noumenon* at the Henry Street Playhouse in New York, he sheathed his dancers in stretch fabric that shrewdly masked the individual's sex (an idea he would return to in one of his key works, *Kaleidoscope*) even as it created "masses" in movement. What was the audience seeing? A dancer or a living sculpture? A genre scene or an abstract study? By subverting the outcome of physical movement, Nikolais challenged audience perception. From work to work he continued to interrogate the representational process, constantly inventive. He appropriated elastic bands to create a geometric ballet that circumscribed movement (*Tensile Movement*, 1955), and he used a Kodak carrousel projector to project pictures on the bodies of his dancers (*Somniloquy*, 1967). In every instance, Nikolais sought to achieve a total theater that merged image, dance, and color. In most cases, he succeeded. His popularity and his aura, fueled by appearances on TV, transcended the second half of the twentieth century. And he found like-minded associates in his partner, Murray Louis, and his muse, Carolyn Carlson.

Nikolais also enjoyed a special relationship with France. He was named director of the Centre National de Danse Contemporaine in Anger, the first of its kind, which he headed from 1978 to 1981. There he discovered a young prodigy named Philippe Decouflé, who never misses an opportunity to remind people of the importance of his mentor. Many people felt that Nikolais's inventive, colorful style never reached the heights attained by Merce Cunningham, but on seeing his choreography performed today by a troupe based on his former dancers, the Ririe Woodbury Dance Company, it is clear that there is still much to be learned from his marvelous universe. Nikolais's innovations did not remain still-born; on the contrary, their ripple effect is still being felt, and not only because many of his associates—including Claudia Gilteman, Carolyn Carlson, and Murray Louis—have followed in his wake even while forging their own paths, but also because, as a terrific teacher, Alwin Nikolais gave others, everywhere, a desire to dance. A dance to be shared, in short.

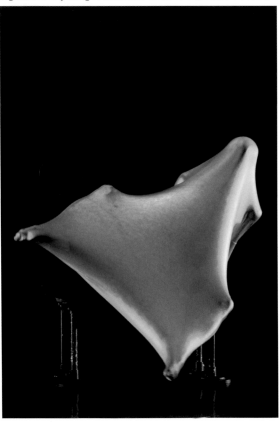

Alwin Nikolais, *Noumenon* (1953).
Noumenon—from the Greek for "I think"—
is a ballet that explores forms with distinct wit.

dynamiting the rules of classical ballet:

WILLIAM FORSYTHE

In theory, this German-based American choreographer should be consigned to an appendix of this book dealing with neoclassical dance or some similar category. Just consider William Forsythe's career: he was a classical dancer who trained at the best schools, went to Europe where he worked with John Cranko in Stuttgart, and then settled down in Frankfurt. His vocabulary was familiar—toe work, academic leotards, pas de deux, ensemble dancing. His early admirers included Rudolf Nureyev, who commissioned a piece for the Paris Opera Ballet as early as 1983, *France/Dance*. Forsythe was viewed as a worthy successor to George Balanchine (the Russian choreographer who worked with Diaghilev's ballet companies before emigrating to the United States where he rejuvenated classical ballet in the latter half of the twentieth century at the New York City Ballet); for that matter, during his first appearances in Paris Forsythe was misleadingly referred to as the (un)worthy heir of "Mister B." But the reinvigoration spearheaded by Forsythe was different: in 1984 he choreographed *Artifact* for the Frankfurt Ballet, a manifesto of a piece that shattered the neoclassical calm. It was full of often astonishing ideas, such as a stage curtain that fragmented the choreography by lowering and rising a unexpected moments, imaginative lighting (by Forsythe himself) that created moving silhouettes on shifting backdrops, snatches of spoken texts (sometimes offbeat), and a non illustrative use of music (from Johann Sebastian Bach to an original score by Eve Crossman Hecht). *Artifact* was a work of pure dance that respected conventional codes of pointe dancing, arabesques, and lifts, yet was simultaneously and above all an exploded opera in which the body became a precision instrument for dismantling theatrical machinery. Alongside the many allusions that reminded audiences of where Forsythe was coming from—namely the classical world— there were also subtexts: as a dancer-cum-choreographer Forsythe acknowledged his love of American musicals, having imagined himself as new Fred Astaire when a boy; while as an adult he turned blithely to philosophy, sidestepping the trap of virtuosity for virtuosity's sake even though his company boasted outstanding technique. Forsythe enjoyed slowing the pace of dance to a majestic series of "choreographic tracking shots." Audiences were stunned as ballet fans felt their traditions slipping away. Advocates of

William Forsythe, *In the Middle, Somewhat Elevated*, (1987).
A pas de deux that plays on the classical register through distinctive armwork.

contemporary dance, however, did not recognize Forsythe as one of their own—yet. In the marvelous decades that followed, Forsythe produced a parody of a musical (*Isabelle's Dance*), a bold choreographic fresco (*Impressing the Czar*), and a few of the finest duets and quartets of the day. He also invented a totally new concept, a kind of ghost- or shadow-dancing where dancers literally and figuratively wrapped themselves in one another. Forsythe constantly called his own work into question, reinventing his company when the Frankfurt Ballet fell victim to budget cuts in 2004. His recent pieces, some of which have political overtones, can still unsettle audiences. As to *Artifact*, in the summer of 2009 it entered the repertoire of the Royal Ballet of Flanders, headed by Kathryn Bennetts, Forsythe's former assistant. Forsythe has been—and remains—one of the few dynamic figures in a dance scene that transcends classical and contemporary, which is no mean feat. In his wake, an entire generation of dancer-choreographers from the classical fold has emerged. Wayne McGregor and Christopher Wheeldon, without copying Forsythe, drew inspiration from the Frankfurt master's deconstruction of classical ballet. Forsythe himself seems to have found the secret of eternal youth in works that hover between performance and installation. One of his key slogans at the premiere of *Artifact*, "Welcome to what you think you see," echoed around the dance world. And is still echoing today.

revolutionizing the body in *parades and changes:*
ANNA HALPRIN

In the United States dance occupies two distinct territories, along an east-west divide. Anna Halprin is based in the San Francisco Bay area on the West Coast, that is to say a long way from New York with its dance studios and famous companies (Merce Cunningham, Paul Taylor, Alvin Ailey). Which meant that in 1965 Halprin was still a well-kept secret of what would be called postmodern dance, even though dancers such as Trisha Brown and Yvonne Rainer went to work with her. Much of the general public is still unfamiliar with Halprin, a seminal figure in the history of American dance. In 1965, she premiered *Parades and Changes* in Stockholm—far from her home base—to music by Morton Subotnick. Two sections of the work, which would later be considered a masterpiece of twentieth-century dance, attracted particular attention. Coming one after another, these two sequences shocked

THEY DARED TO DO IT

audiences. First, dancers arrived on stage wearing a "uniform" of white shirt and dark pants, only to undress ("Dressing and Undressing"); then, they began a "Paper Dance" wearing only large pieces of paper that progressively tore, revealing the dancers' full anatomy. Never before in dance had nudity been so raw—or so much fun. Although *Parades and Changes* should not be reduced to these two sequences alone, they were certainly at the roots of its scandalous reputation.

When the piece was revived some time later, it enjoyed a short run in Los Angeles and San Francisco, but the director of the Museum of Contemporary Art in San Francisco was wary of scandal and prior to the performance asked Halprin if she would consider asking the dancers to don underwear. The most uninhibited choreographer of the day replied, half-amused, half-weary: "OK, as long as you put stickers over all the nudes in your museum." She carried her point, and *Parades and Changes* was performed uncensored, including the famous undressing scene. In New York, however, the piece created a scandal that earned Halprin a conviction for indecency and prevented performance of the ballet for twenty years.

It was in France that this pioneering ballet began to be revived in 2004. For Halprin the important thing wasn't eroticism, but authentic dance based on improvisation. Behind this partial revival—as well as the full reinterpretation in 2008—were dancers and choreographers Alain Buffard and Anne Collod. Buffard pointed out just how far in advance of its times *Parade and Changes* really was. Long before anyone else Halprin introduced notions of androgyny (with which contemporary dance would make hay—forty years later) and employed rhythms such as stomp dancing. *Parade and Changes Replay* (the clever title of the revived version) was thus launched on a new career. Halprin, still somewhat orphaned in her own country, has now found a larger family—the family of dance.

Anna Halprin, *Parades and Changes* (1965–67),
Parades and Changes Replay (2008).
Halprin's masterpiece created a scandal when first performed
in America, but is enjoying a second life in the twenty-first century.

dancing in concert:
ANNE TERESA DE KEERSMAEKER

The relationship between dance and music is a whole subject in itself. An entire book could be devoted to it, covering periods of harmony and incomprehension, offering portraits of great composers (from Tchaikovsky to Stravinsky, in short) and choreographers with keenly attuned ears. Such a book would have to include Anne Teresa De Keersmaeker, the most influential of Belgian choreographers. Keersmaeker enjoyed a broad background, ranging from the famous Mudra school to the Tisch School of the Arts at New York University. In her first "incarnation," the dancer used and abused repetitive techniques: *Fase*, which brought her recognition in 1982, was based on a score by American minimalist composer Steve Reich and hinged on dance phrases repeated in loop fashion by a virtuoso duo composed of Michèle-Anne de Mey and De Keersmaeker herself. In addition to a distinct style, this

piece featured dancers wearing schoolgirl shoes and dresses that reveal their underwear, creating an unusual look on stage.

Soon, however, De Keersmaeker began focusing on "seeing music" and "listening to dance." She pushed this principle to an extreme in *Mikrokosmos* (1987), a triptych composed of two parts dance separated by one part music—a concert with live musicians on stage, all performed in a single evening. The music of Béla Bartók and György Ligeti provided the linking thread. There was some incomprehension among the audience, which could not understand how movement could come to a halt, yielding to static listening. Through force of conviction, however, De Keersmaeker has managed to achieve her ends. Her "dance concerts" are now an established fact—and a success. But beyond this new staging, it is dance's relationship to music that has moved the goal lines. The presence of musicians—such as a pianist or string ensemble—became a creative mechanism not only for De Keersmaeker but also for other choreographers in the 1990s. With another of her poorly understood shows, the forceful *Ottone Ottone* (1988), Keersmaeker revitalized opera, turning it into malleable sound material: each dancer incarnated a voice, without however slavishly illustrating Monteverdi's score of *The Coronation of Poppea*.

In 2009 De Keersmaeker headed in yet another direction, incorporating noise rather than music into her ballet *The Song*. She who conscientiously played the flute as a child admitted that she no longer knew which composer to look to, "which music was required for this piece."* Which led to a first, free-falling phase of repetitive movements in silence as De Keersmaeker turned this new interrelationship between body, movement, and sound into the driving force behind *The Song*, a fierce masterpiece. "Dance concerts" were thus succeeded by movements "dubbed" by a sound-effects engineer. With almost nothing—some water, some paper—De Keersmaeker herself composed, live, the sound track to dance conceived as free flight.

Anne Teresa De Keersmaeker, *D'un soir un jour* (A Day in a Night, 2006). An unusually moving ballet based on six pieces of music by three composers (Debussy, Stravinsky, and Benjamin).

Le Monde, (2009).

CHRISTIAN RIZZO ✷ *ni fleurs, ni ford mustang* (No Flowers or Mustangs, Please, 2004), Lyon Opera Ballet

DANCE AND THE CIRCUS

A three-ring circus of unexpected consequences might be the brief description of the marriage of (in)convenience between contemporary dance and modern circus, which has enjoyed a revival in the past two decades. From circus shows staged by choreographers to the growing presence of circus performers in ballets with shifting forms, this particular pas de deux has become a headliner.

The relatively new art of "modern circus shows" has enjoyed steady growth in France, reinforced by unanticipated media coverage since the mid-1990s. Apart from veteran circus troupes led by Dromesko and Bartabas—the latter having made his name with an equestrian theater company, Zingaro, closely in step with dance—today's circus shows tend to eschew animals. Most acts feature humans on trapeze, trampoline, or high wire, or performing feats of juggling. With which dance could hardly find fault.

In fact, the trend (re)commenced in France at the Centre National des Arts du Cirque (CNAC), founded in Châlons-en-Champagne in 1985. It was a first in Europe. Ten years later, coordination of the end-of-year show was handed over to a highly theatrical choreographer, Josef Nadj, who produced *Le cri du Caméléon* (Cry of the Chameleon, 1995). Bingo. Relying solely on CNAC students, Nadj insisted on a frontal format (artists directly facing the audience, rather than ringed by spectators) and on the presence of circus performers throughout the piece. He also stressed his own colorful idiom: performers juggled with hats, slid across the floor, leaped into the air, and did a series of high-speed leaps. Music and costumes were reminiscent of Nadj's previous pieces, somewhere between burlesque melancholy and Slavic soul. "In fact, I don't work differently with circus performers," says Nadj, "even though I know their training favors exploits.... They can attain new limits, which is very interesting because you can access a world of marvels where the impossible becomes possible." *Le cri du Caméléon* was a total hit and toured the world. People began to look forward to CNAC's end-of-year show with anticipation. Its trademark virtuosity and inventiveness was often choreographic. Guest choreographers who spent time at CNAC, with greater or lesser success, included François Verret, Francesca Lattuada, Philippe Decouflé, Héla Fattoumi and Éric Lamoureux, Fatou Traoré, and Jean-Claude Gallotta (in conjunction with Georges Levaudant from the theatrical world). Above all the circus students, many of whom were encountering contemporary dance for the first time, had their minds opened, which facilitated cross-fertilization. Today many circus performers,

whether contortionists or acrobats, participate in dance events. The likes of Jean-Baptiste André, Mathurin Bolze, and Angela Laurier "dance" in their own way for choreographers such as François Verret and Christian Rizzo. Or else dance for themselves in new hybrid forms of show. A clownish André juggles with a sly microphone in *Comme en plein jour* (Looks Like Daylight); Bolze encounters his "twin," Hedi Thabet, in *Ali*; and Laurier recounts her sometimes disturbing family history in *Déversoir* (Overflow) and *J'aimerais pouvoir rire!* (I'd Like to Laugh!). The once-vaunted physical feat in circus is no longer a goal in itself; instead, the body is used to generate emotion. And audiences love it. Belgian choreographers Alain Platel and Koen Augustijnen from the C de la B collective, as well as Sidi Larbi Cherkaoui, have enrolled circus artists in their latest shows. Suddenly a performer may drop from the flies hanging from a long piece of cloth (in Platel's *vsprs* and *Pitié*) while others play with and straddle long flexible poles (Cherkaoui's *Tempus Fugit* and *Myth*). Again and again, the summits of the dance and circus worlds seem to converge.

In the United States, an uncategorizable artist like Elizabeth Streb with her Streb Extreme Action troupe daringly combines risky leaps with danced movement. In one Streb daredevil number a helmeted performer crashed through a wall of glass. Streb not only produces shows, she also organizes events for kids and disadvantaged folks. Finally, some hip-hop artists such as Mourad Merzouki with his *Terrain vague* (Vacant Lot) have casually—and successfully—incorporated circus techniques.

It would be remiss not to mention the extraordinary circus artists who also merit the title of choreographer. From work to work, James Thierrée, grandson of Charlie Chaplin, has transformed acrobatics into perfect arabesques. In *La symphonie du hanneton* (The May Bug Symphony) he invented a marvelous world of weightlessness, as he did in his solo piece, *Raoul*. Aurélien Bory's Compagnie 111 included circus performers in *Plus ou moins l'infini* (The Infinite, More or Less) and recruited Chinese artists from the Dalian Circus for *Les sept planches de la ruse* (Seven Plates of Guile), which combined the rigor of the circus

François Verret,
Kaspar Konzert (1998).
A leading contemporary
choreographer, Verret
looked to the circus arts
when seeking a new
take on the body.

Martin Zimmermann
and Dimitri de Perrot,
Öper Öpis (2008).
This Swiss pair performs
a balancing act to create
a weightless dance with
striking images and a live
mix of music tracks.

with the emotion of dance. As to the Swiss pair
Zimmermann and Perrot, one trained at CNAC and the
other performed as a musician; they startle audiences
with bold concoctions in which circus numbers alternate
with danced sequences or free movement, as seen in *Öper
Öpis*. **Tartuffe's Mr. Loyal can rest easy—dance is
not about to evict the circus.**

ABOVE

Josef Nadj, *Le cri du Caméléon* (The Cry of the Chameleon, 1995). Students from a circus school brought their agility to Nadj's dark humor. The upshot was a smash hit.

FACING PAGE

James Thierrée, *Raoul* (2009). In a wonderful set designed by his mother, Victoria Chaplin-Thierrée, the choreographer's galloping imagination took off on a long voyage.

DANCE AND THE VISUAL ARTS

Flirting with the fine arts doesn't mean forcing dance into a framework, much less turning ballet into a pretty picture. Rather, it brings Terpsichore, the muse of song and dance, face to face with painting and sculpture. This fruitful encounter was begun back in the days of the Diaghilev's Ballets Russes and Rolf de Maré's Ballets Suédois. Although it has not always been easy, the connection has consistently enriched the contemporary art.

Whether coincidental or not, it was in the revolutionary year of 1968 that Merce Cunningham presented *Walkaround Time* as a tribute to one of the most influential artists of the twentieth century, Marcel Duchamp. In a set by the Jasper Johns, a master of Pop Art in the United States, Cunningham notably paid homage to a key Duchamp painting of 1912, *Nude Descending a Staircase*. With respect to Duchamp, Cunningham said that he was inspired by the inventor of readymades but hadn't copied anything—the inspiration was movement itself, not ideas for movement. Many years earlier, Duchamp had made a personal appearance in *Relâche* (No Performance Today), a ballet by his friends Picabia and Satie, commissioned by the Ballets Suédois in 1924. For that matter Cunningham, the serene leader of the American choreographic revolution, regularly worked with fine artists of his day. Robert Rauschenberg, Frank Stella, and, more recently, Ernesto Neto have done the sets or stage environments. Sometimes the décor consists of painted flats or sculptural objects that do not interfere with the dance. Bolder was *Rainforest* (1968), where two very famous universes collided: those of Cunningham and Andy Warhol, the pope of Pop Art, who in a one-off effort (he is not known to have contributed to any other dance piece), filled the stage with helium-inflated silver cushions that sprang into movement at the mere presence of Cunningham's dancers; there ensued an astonishingly graceful double choreography for humans and objects, totally in the Warhol spirit. Other American choreographers from Trisha Brown to Karole Armitage would later work with the likes of Rauschenberg (for Brown's superb *Set and Reset*) and Jeff Koons (Armitage's *Go-Go Ballerina*).

In Europe, on the heels of the masters Maurice Béjart and Roland Petit, who regularly looked to the visual artists, a new generation of choreographers got in on the act. Angelin Preljocaj first called upon Aki Kuroda for a program devoted to the Ballets Russes, then upon radical artist Fabrice Hyber for a very colorful *4 Saisons* (4 Seasons) in which Hyber installed a hanging rail along which paraded sculptural forms derived from his own POFs (Prototypes of Objects

that Function), as well as costumes in the shape of a plastic bear and day-glo green virus.

In 1993, Odile Duboc, a great if discreet dame of French dance who passed away in 2010, presented *Projet de la matière* (Material Project), in which she collaborated with artist Marie-José Pillet. Pillet designed highly effective props such as a soft object that wed the shape of the dancers' bodies and a sloping metallic platform that captured the energy of footwork. Hervé Robbe, who studied architecture before moving into dance, now designs installations in which dance and video cohabit. Above all, Robbe convinced British sculptor Richard Deacon to set up a *Factory* (1993), the title of a subtle piece of dance; amid Deacon's round, see-sawing sculptures, Robbe devised an organic vocabulary of movement that excites the senses, inviting the audience to experience the work like the dance, by moving freely among it.

Régine Chopinot has constantly favored a dialogue with visual artists, from Jean Le Gac to Jean-Michel Bruyère. *Vegetal* (1995) is perhaps one of the highpoints of her multifaceted oeuvre. For this piece she brought together land artist Andy Goldsworthy and fifteen dancers. In a long ritual that predated the ecology movement, performers come and go on stage, bringing branches with which they built an ephemeral, Goldsworthy-like sculpture, thereby making an artwork themselves.

FACING PAGE (TOP)
Trisha Brown, *Floor of the Forest* (1970). This installation was composed of a weave of garments that the dancers had to don. It was subsequently performed at

Documenta 12 in Kassel, Germany, as well as at the Pompidou Center and the Tuileries Gardens (pictured here) in Paris.

FACING PAGE (BOTTOM)
Odile Duboc, *Projet de la matière* (Material Project, 1993). The dancers must deal with "soft" sculptures and other—harder—objects created by the artist Marie-José Pillet.

DANCE AND FASHION

Because it is a question of bodies, you might think that dance and fashion go together naturally. Except for one detail. On stage, far from the catwalk, dancers move frantically, clutch their partners, roll on the floor, sweat, and so on. So designers have to come up with garments that are not so much wearable as danceable. No easy matter.

Apart from rare exceptions, dancers have always required costumes. So it was inevitable that dance and fashion would meet one day. And yet a look at the history of choreography shows a distinctive reticence in the matter. First of all, there was the tradition of theatrical costume designers who did not want to let "the fashion crowd" grab all the limelight. And then there were the constraints inherent to dance, an art of movement that requires specific design skills. And apart from basic design, any garment worn on stage has to be practical and very sturdy. One of the first fashion designers to take the leap was none other than Coco Chanel, who in the early twentieth century designed sober if sporty costumes made notably of jersey knits for the *Le train bleu* (The Mediterranean Express) by the Ballets Russes. Chanel, who was friends with Stravinsky and Diaghilev, as well as an art patron in her spare time, realized that she had to efface her own work to the benefit of the performer.

A number of successful attempts at fashion collaboration occurred in the latter half of the twentieth century. Maurice Béjart with Gianni Versace, Roland Petit with Yves Saint Laurent, Martha Graham with Calvin Klein and Halston. But it has been contemporary dance that has gone furthest down the path. True enough, the rise of luxury ready-to-wear, which is more affordable than haute couture, had a notable impact on expanding the portrait gallery of fashion designers. The likes of Paul Poiret, Christian Dior, and Hubert de Givenchy were replaced on the covers of fashion mags by Jean-Paul Gaultier, Christian Lacroix, Issey Miyake, and Rei Kawakubo (Comme des Garçons), among others. Gaultier, the darling of fashion editors, was the designer who pushed his flirtation with dance the furthest, first with Régine Chopinot, the French choreographer from La Rochelle who was a star of the 1980s. The pair's masterwork was, of course, titled *Le défilé* (The Fashion Show), an ironic and irreverent tribute to the world of fashion: dancers and other invited performers paraded along a catwalk in costumes of outrageous inventiveness (XL underpants, a Marie-Antoinette-style knitted dress for the third millennium, a jacket with a picture frame built into it, etc.).

This fashionable triumph echoed far beyond the narrow world of dance. The fruitful collaboration between Gaultier, whose star continued to rise, and Chopinot was punctuated by dance-and-fashion events. *Kok* was danced on a ring in rejigged athletic gear, *ANA* employed padded weights and mirror effects, *Façade* unveiled one-piece jumpsuits that even covered the face (a little too completely, as it transpired: the dancers had difficulty breathing). The pair have subsequently followed their own paths. In 2008, Gaultier worked with Angelin Preljocaj on a new-look *Blanche Neige* (Snow White); his Catwoman-like stepmother wore a vinyl outfit, while his monkish dwarves wore leather shorts that called for severe correction—Gaultier, who henceforth devoted himself to haute couture, used everything that came to hand.

The simultaneously baroque and classical Christian Lacroix turned more toward ballet. He nevertheless gave free rein to whimsy in *Zoopsie Comedy*, a highly contemporary work inspired by cabaret fashion, revived in a new version by Dominique Boivin and Dominique Rebaud, two whimsical choreographers.

The more radical Japanese designer Rei Kawakubo amazed people by joining up with Merce Cunningham for *Scenario*. Stretch pants and dresses in green, red, and black check were enlivened with various protuberances. When the dancers leaped in the air, these wrappers of unlabeled origin revealed artistically mutant bodies. Another Japanese designer, Issey Miyake, worked first with Béjart before coming across William Forsythe. Miyake's line of Pleats Please, involving a technique that folded stretch fabrics like works of origami, were worn by the dancers of Forsythe's Frankfurt ballet. The designer then put on a show of his own work that was modeled by the same dancers. Following these encounters, some of which became marriages of inconvenience as far as the dancers are concerned, other designers joined the procession, such as Dries van Noten (with Anne Teresa De Keersmaeker), Alexander McQueen (with Russell Maliphant), and Marc Jacobs (with Benjamin Millepied). **A pas de deux that is always prêt-à-danser.**

BELOW
Régine Chopinot,
ANA (1990).
Jean-Paul Gaultier's
wonderful neo-tutus
and polka-dot leotards
are a perfect
complement to
Chopinot's playful
choreography.

LEFT
Merce Cunningham,
Scenario (1997),
Merce Cunningham
Dance Company.
Rei Kawakubo, the Japanese
designer for Comme des
Garçons, concocted these
"deformed" costumes from
a stretch fabric that
combined comfort with
technical performance.

FOLLOWING PAGES
Régine Chopinot/
Jean-Paul Gaultier, *Le défilé*
(Fashion Show, 1985).
Wool crinoline made for an
unforgettable collection.

DANCE AND OPERA

If any partnership is stormy, it's certainly the one between dance and opera. The latter, which many people consider to be a "total artwork," has often looked upon dance with a touch of condescension. Since the choreographic art traditionally played a bit part rather than a leading role, it has had trouble breaking into the limelight.

There still exists a tradition of ballet within opera. In Germany, for example, many classical ballet companies are still under the wing of opera houses, which are greedier when it comes to personnel, budget, rehearsal time, and occupation of the stage. Thus when the then little-known William Forsythe became head of the Frankfurt Ballet, he hastened to divorce it from the lyric operations in order to gain greater autonomy. On another level, when Pina Bausch inherited the Wuppertal Ballet it was somewhat down-at-heel, and she had to work hard to make it a landmark company.

In France at the end of the twentieth century there were still a few companies linked to opera houses in Nice and Avignon, which put on a handful of ballets per year and participated in lighter opera fare. **Yet it still requires boldness for choreographers to impose themselves as directors of operatic works—they have less margin of error than other directors. So those choreographers who have managed to reconcile the two forms of art, at least for a while, deserve all the greater attention.**

A choreographer such as Trisha Brown, whose career was based on American postmodern dance, might not seem the best candidate to direct an opera. And yet her *Orfeo*, with music conducted by René Jacobs, was one of the most dazzling hits of its kind. Brown had already choreographed a *Carmen* directed by Lina Wertmüller, and explored Bach's *Musical Offering* in M.O. But with Monteverdi's *Orfeo* in 1998 she was in sole charge for the première in Brussels. Her genius lay in creating a constantly harmonious weave between dancing, singing, and acting. The vocal cast seem to move better than ever, while a dancer clinging to a rope floated around the set—choreography was not a counterpoint to the action, it *was* the action. Conceived from the start by a specialist, the choreographic language became an extension of the singing. Brown went on to direct *Luci mie traditrici* and *Da gelo a gelo* by Salvatore Sciarrino and will perhaps produce both opera and ballet versions of Jean-Philippe Rameau's *Pygmalion*.

Baroque works, in fact, have reconciled many opera lovers to dance. Much credit should be given to *Atys*, a newly revived score of courtly French music by Lully, composer to Louis XIV. In a production that had a big impact at the time, it was revived some years ago by choral conductor William Christie, stage director Jean-Marie Villégier, and choreographer and researcher Francine Lancelot. Lancelot, who studied under Mary Wigman in Germany and the Dupuys in France, reconstructed dance steps that were a revelation to all. She also invented other steps. Thanks to her company, Ris et Danceries, there was a revival in France of baroque art that often combined dance and opera. Now deceased, Lancelot trained "students" such as Geneviève Massé and Béatrice Massin. The latter's works—such as *Que ma joie demeure* (May My Joy Last) and *Songes* (Daydreams)—are moreover delightful tributes to baroque operatic airs.

Perhaps somewhat more iconoclastic, the duo of José Montalvo and Dominique Hervieu have given new life Rameau's opera *Les Paladins* by imposing their own sense of tempo and startling visual juxtapositions (meticulous gardens and jungle animals). They also juxtapose various dance forms, from classical to contemporary to hip-hop. Although the opera was turned upside down, audiences loved it. The pair repeated the experiment in a more contemporary, indeed political, vein, with George Gershwin's *Porgy and Bess*.

The siren song of opera has also been heard by the German Sasha Waltz, a passed master in the art of creating worlds where the stage set can become more important than the dance steps. *Dido and Aeneas* was conceived as a total artwork combining song, acting, and dance—the long-separated lovers were even plunged into a giant "aquarium." When commissioned by the Paris Opera to produce Berlioz's *Roméo et Juliette* (2007), Waltz pushed the vocalists into a physical exercise close to choreography, while the dancers had to play with a shifting set that symbolized the tragedy that befell the lovers of Verona.

Far from the glitter of opera, it is worth mentioning *Wolf*, an exemplary production by Flemish choreographer Alain Platel, which premiered in an abandoned industrial site in

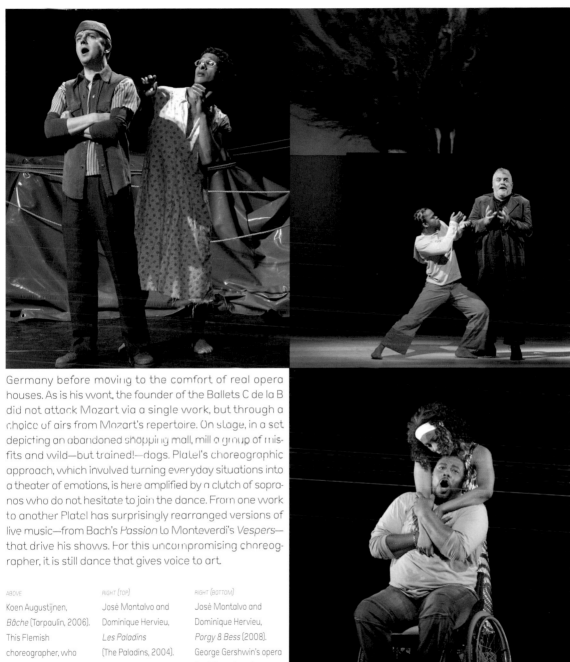

Germany before moving to the comfort of real opera houses. As is his wont, the founder of the Ballets C de la B did not attack Mozart via a single work, but through a choice of airs from Mozart's repertoire. On stage, in a set depicting an abandoned shopping mall, mill a group of misfits and wild—but trained!—dogs. Platel's choreographic approach, which involved turning everyday situations into a theater of emotions, is here amplified by a clutch of sopranos who do not hesitate to join the dance. From one work to another Platel has surprisingly rearranged versions of live music—from Bach's *Passion* to Monteverdi's *Vespers*—that drive his shows. For this uncompromising choreographer, it is still dance that gives voice to art.

ABOVE

Koen Augustijnen, *Bâche* (Tarpaulin, 2006). This Flemish choreographer, who got his start with Ballets C. de la B., likes to make dance sing.

RIGHT (TOP)

José Montalvo and Dominique Hervieu, *Les Paladins* (The Paladins, 2004). Jean-Baptiste Rameau's baroque opera here becomes an imagistic fable.

RIGHT (BOTTOM)

José Montalvo and Dominique Hervieu, *Porgy & Bess* (2008). George Gershwin's opera for African-Americans was directed and choreographed by this French pair.

DANCE AND PERFORMANCE ART

It was in the United States that dance hitched up with performance art in a clear—and acknowledged—desire for osmosis. By experimenting with new forms of representation and by working with ultimately ordinary materials, the bodily marriage of dance and performance art produced some of the finest chapters in twentieth-century creative art. But will it have any heirs?

If we had to pick one date that symbolized the union, it would probably be July 6, 1962. On that day a dance recital was given in the Judson Church in New York. The performers had all attended a workshop given by Robert Dunn, a former student of John Cage, held in Merce Cunningham's studio. The people who performed in the show over three (long) hours were dancers ranging from Trisha Brown and David Gordon to Deborah Hay and Steve Paxton. And during their sessions with Dunn they met musicians such as Terry Riley and La Monte Young and visual artists such as Robert Morris. They communally shared their performance experiments that questioned both the gaze of the beholder and the stage itself as a site of artistic production. Over the years, these dance performances would take different forms, performed on wall or roof (*Roof* by Trisha Brown, 1971), and would give rise to the postmodern movement. Although they never reached a wide audience, they had a marked influence on succeeding generations of choreographers on both sides of the Atlantic. Above all, live dance would invade museums, art galleries, parking lots, and quite simply the street.

The late twentieth century was punctuated by these encounters between dance and performance art. One of the most fascinating and successful experiments was carried out by William Forsythe, an American choreographer based in Frankfurt, Germany. Trained as a dancer of classical ballet—whose foundations he deliberately undermined—Forsythe became a creative contemporary choreographer thanks to his solid background, and went on to delve in performance art, hitting the streets with giant balloons on which live images were projected, or occupying a gallery of the Louvre in a distant tribute to Francis Bacon. Above all, in *Heterotopia* (2007), Forsythe invoked the "figure" of Michel Foucault through a shed of a set cut in two, an audience that moved around, an invented language, and simultaneous actions, all resulting in a deconstructed yet fascinating masterpiece.

Some choreographers have gone further in the mixing of genres. Maria La Ribot from Spain presents her *Piezas distinguadas* as longer or shorter modules combined to make a show that may last four hours or an entire day. The dancer's body, often naked, is the vehicle for this concept in motion. Meanwhile, a former rocker and dancer like Christian Rizzo approached the spirit of performance art in his practically motionless ballets in which dancers "perform" more than dance. In *Autant vouloir le bleu du ciel et m'en aller sur un âne* (May as Well Seek the Blue of the Sky and Leave on a Donkey, 2004) Rizzo smeared his face with tiny beads, creating an improvised mask of blinding beauty as he moved among folding screens. In another, large-scale performance piece, *Avant un mois je serai revenu et nous irons ensemble en matinée tu sais, voir la comédie où je t'ai promis de te conduire* (I'll Come Back Before the Month is Out and We'll Go, You Know, to a Matinee of that Play I Promised to Take You To, 2002), the

unusually slow action on stage cast this non-spectacle as a dazzling tableau vivant of immaculate whiteness; inspired by artists such as James Lee Byars, Rizzo seeks to weave a new spell within his own universe.

Alain Buffard, another figure of performance dance of the 1990s, went so far as to recreate, on stage, an event by American artist Vito Acconci, *INtime/EXtime*. In *Good Boy*, a solo that explicitly deals with illness, Buffard put on then took off white underpants, while making improvised high heels from boxes of medication. He has summed up his idea by saying that what interests him in the body and the medium of dance "is their multiplicity, the sole truly open road toward transformation." The involuntary leader of a brand new generation of dancer-performers, Buffard has "discovered" talents such as the duo of François Chaignaud and Cecilia Bengolea, who concoct an unsettling visual realm from glass jars and latex jumpsuits.

In a more classic vein, and with an execution that verges on perfection, Josef Nadj premiered *Paso Doble* with Spanish painter Miquel Barceló at the 2006 Avignon festival. Playing with a curved wall of clay, the two men wallow in the material of a dance that allows them to invent malleable—sculptural—bodies. Nadj, like Cunningham a draftsman in his spare time, is also close to performance art in the line-drawn *Last Landscape*, which looks as though it was sketched from life.

If we had to uncover a fairy godmother for the marriage of performance and dance, it would certainly be the fine artist Marina Abramovic. In an encounter with Jan Fabre and the Palais de Tokyo in Paris, the pair donned armor and shut themselves into a glass cage. And they let movement, made sluggish through the weight of their vestments, speak for itself.

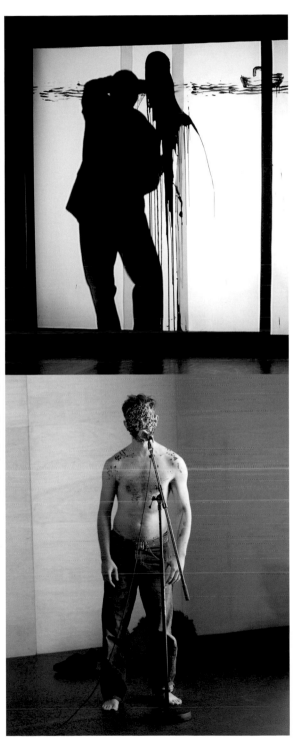

FACING PAGE
Josef Nadj/Miquel Barceló, *Paso Doble* (2006).
A highly physical piece in which both performers become engulfed in clay.
RIGHT (TOP)
Josef Nadj, *Last Landscape* (2005, first version), *Paysage après l'orage* (Landscape

After the Storm, 2006, second version).
A self-portrait of the artist in a pure solo.
RIGHT (BOTTOM)
Christian Rizzo, *Autant vouloir le bleu du ciel et m'en aller sur un âne* (May as Well Seek the Blue of the Sky and Leave on a Donkey, 2004).

Rizzo here turns his own body into an artwork, his face into a precious mask.
FOLLOWING PAGES
William Forsythe, *Yes We Can't* (2008).
Playing on both words and dance, Forsythe plunders Obama's famous campaign slogan.

30 DANCERS/CHOREOGRAPHERS

9

30 DANCERS/CHOREOGRAPHERS

USHIO AMAGATSU

his background

Born in 1949, Ushio Amagatsu has been a leading figure of postwar Japanese creativity and was one of the founders of the Dairakuda-kan collective in 1972. In the following eight years Amagatsu contributed to the troupe's new pieces under the aegis of Maro Akaji, who had worked with Tatsumi Hijikata, the inventor of the unique movement known as Butoh. Amagatsu, who had studied classical and modern dance, went on to found his own "dance" company, Sankai Juku, which could be translated as "studio by the mountain and the sea." Early works such as *Amagatsu Shō* and *Shoriba* steadily developed a new vision of the body, but it was *Kinkan Shonen* (The Kumquat Seed) in 1978 that first brought Amagatsu international renown: the vision of men whose rice-powdered faces made them seem unisex altered Western perceptions of dance theater.

Amagatsu regularly presented new pieces in which he himself performed. But in 1985 a tragic event, the death of a dancer hanging by his feet during a Sankai Juku open-air performance air, probably signaled the end of his total commitment to Butoh-type work. Today Amagatsu's pieces are rituals of a nearly perfect visual beauty that find their "natural" setting in theaters. Time seems to leave no mark on Amagatsu himself, who divides his creative career between Paris and Tokyo.

his style

In *Kinkan Shonen*, a masterpiece that is still performed throughout the world today, Amagatsu rolled back time through the conceit of a "child" who imagines himself to be a fish. This piece has aged well; Amagatsu has only just handed the reins to three disciple-dancers who have recreated his original role in a slow, beautiful ceremony set among dried fish. From one work to the next, enlightened fans quickly become familiar with the Sankai Juku vocabulary: slow movements, bodies like reeds that bend but never break, and much floor work (often in the choreographer's favored fetal position). Above all, the impressive mastery of stage sets that are simultaneously mineral and organic convey the full measure of Amagatsu's art, whether featuring giant eggs (*Unestu*, 1986), basins filled with a bloody liquid (*Hibiki*, 1998), or seven tall stones raised during the show (*Toki*, 2005). On stage, solos often alternate with ensemble passages performed solely by men.

In 2007 Amagatsu was commissioned by Indian dancer Shantala Shivalingappa to choreograph a solo for her. The result, *Ibaku*, was of a rare beauty far from the grotesque, occasionally sexually specific language of the original Butoh. A refined moment.

"When we dance in a theater we unite time and space between dancer and audience. In this respect, dance is also a ceremony."

Ushio Amagatsu/Sankai Juku, *Tobari* (2008).

PINA BAUSCH

Pina Bausch, *Kontakthof with Young People Fourteen or Over* (revival, 2008).

"**You have to learn to let yourself be touched by beauty, by a gesture or hint of inspiration, not just by what is said, in whatever language. You have to perceive independently of everything you 'know.' You have to judge without knowing!**"

her background

Born in Solingen in the Ruhr region of Germany in 1940, Philippine (Pina) Bausch first studied dance at the school in Essen run by Kurt Jooss. Then she attended the Juilliard School in New York—without speaking a word of English, she later claimed. Although she performed in various American companies, she decided to return to Essen. In the late 1960s she choreographed her own works and by 1973 was invited to head the then-declining Wuppertal Ballet. She produced versions of "danced operas" such as Gluck's *Iphigénie en Tauride* and *Orphée et Eurydice*. Little by little, however, she abandoned this neoclassicism for more contemporary, original works in which dancers notably spoke lines. Thus the Tanztheater (dance theater) concept that emerged in the early twentieth century was reborn under the aegis of Bausch, who subsequently influenced dozens of choreographers. The best examples of her early—sometimes tumultuous—shows in Wuppertal are *Bandoneon* and *Arien*. Her death in the summer of 2009 sent shock waves through the dance world and beyond—one of the greatest artists of the day had passed away.

her style

Excluding her earliest pieces (which displayed lyrical beauty but were still under post-classical influence), Bausch developed her style over time: by incorporating texts (not so much improvised as worked out in the studio through a series of questions and answers), and by dividing her ballets into short scenes that follow one another with an innate sense of rhythm, she established the foundations of a dance theater that had a lot to say about real-life feelings and vicissitudes. It evoked stories of couples, of passion and betrayal, and of childhood memories; Bausch wrote herself into *Café Müller*, allegedly based on the interior of her parents' café in Solingen. Everything underscored the dramatic art that subtends Bausch's shows. Once you add remarkable set designers (Rolf Borzik, followed by Peter Pabst) and a highly recognizable wardrobe (long dresses for women, suits for men), then you have the Pina Bausch signature. Carried by outstanding performers gleaned from everywhere on the planet, Bausch's choreography combined round dances, processions, and mad dashes. Solos in which Bausch notably deployed her arms were included in *tableaux-vivant* ballets ranging from *Nelken* (Carnations) and *Der Fensterputzer* (The Window Washer) to *Agua* (Water) and *Wiesenland*. There is less violence in these latter pieces marked by nostalgia and gentleness, sometimes conceived following a residence abroad (India, Korea, Japan, Turkey). But the sharpness of her choreographic vision has been confirmed by two revivals of her dazzling work *Kontakhof*, first with elderly performers and then again with teenagers.

Pina Bausch, *Der Fensterputzer* (The Window Washer, 1997).

JÉRÔME BEL

his background

Is Jérôme Bel an apostle of the "art of modest means" that emerged in the 1990s? Not necessarily. Born in 1964, Bel was a gifted student who trained at the Centre de Danse Contemporaine in Angers, France, before dancing with various companies headed by the likes of Angelin Preljocaj, Bouvier/Obadia, Daniel Larrieu, and Caterina Sagna. In 1992 Bel assisted Philippe Decouflé in staging the exceptional event of the opening ceremony of the Winter Olympic Games in Albertville, France. He then took two "sabbatical" years to ponder, in his own witty way, the "society of the spectacle" and various practices related to a dancer's body. His first work already contained more speech than dance, and was soberly titled *Nom donné par l'auteur* (Name Given by Author). Soon Bel's anti-spectacular approach to movement won him a Europe-wide reputation—along with criticism that he sometimes had difficulty swallowing. Over the years Bel's oeuvre, simultaneously a critique of and a tribute to dance—from classical to contemporary—has encountered unparalleled resonance among young performers. Today he boasts an influence that extends far beyond the world of dance because he is recognized as one of the most original figures on the visual-arts scene, having participated in the 2007 Lyon Biennial of Contemporary Art. Finally, Bel won a prestigious Bessie Award in New York for his most successful work to date, *The Show Must Go On*.

his style

Bel is obviously not a choreographer like the others—indeed, is he really one at all? He does bring dancers—and sometimes actors—on stage, but not for a virtuoso performance; rather, with a view to a study of representation. Bel claims that "over the past fifteen years [his] work has continuously undermined the edifice on which many audiences have structured their relationship to art." The T-shirts donned by the performers in *Shirtology* (1997)—whether solo or in ensemble—function as so many subliminal messages. In *The Show Must Go On*, the presence of the performers and the DJ incarnate the very substance of the soundtrack with its familiar tunes from the world of pop; this piece created a scandal when first staged at the Théâtre de la Ville in Paris, but wound up winning acclaim the world over. It entered the repertoire of the Deutsches Schauspielhaus in Hamburg, and is still on the repertoire of the Lyon Opera Ballet. Finally, in a series of highly affectionate dance-portraits, Bel has staged special works for Véronique Doisneau (with the Paris Opera Ballet), Isabel Torres (with the Teatro Municipal in Rio de Janeiro), and Cédric Andrieux (formerly with Merce Cunningham), all based on the principle of personal accounts by the performer combined with Bel's distanced perspective. Finally, since 2008 nine films on Bel's work (either straightforward records or commentaries) can be accessed on the site www.catalogueraisonne-jeromebel.com—a "virtual" first.

"I think it's the spectators who make the spectacles, they're the ones who fill in the gaps, who project. I don't express anything, I just organize the spectator's subjectivity."

Jérôme Bel, *Le dernier spectacle* (The Last Show, 1998).

BRUNO BELTRÃO

"Il doit y avoir une autre solution"

Défaut : Jaloux

Bruno Beltrão, *Telesquat* (2005).

"I think creating means entering a territory where it's impossible to stay safe."

his background

Born in Niteroi, outside Rio de Janeiro, Brazil, in 1980, Bruno Beltrão began to perform hip-hop, the urban dance par excellence, at the age of nine. As a precocious—and handsome—young talent, Beltrão moved into higher gear at age sixteen by founding the Grupo de Rua de Niteroi with a partner, Rodrigo Bernardi. Beltrão earned his stripes by deploying all available resources, from street battle to reality TV. He also studied art history and philosophy. Things hotted up even more once he won an award in Naples and toured with the Circo de Madrugada, headed by Pierrot Bidon. In 2001 he won recognition among contemporary choreographers for his new work, *From Poping to Pop or Vice Versa*. Subsequently hailed by international critics, Beltrão has been invited to participate in prestigious events such as the Festival d'Automne in Paris, the Kunsten Festival in Brussels, and the Pina Bausch Dance Festival.

his style

Beltrão is one of the most exciting representatives of a still-new genre, hip-hop, which he has progressively stripped of its codified forms in order to transform it into an autonomous dance form. As he has stated and repeated from interview to interview, Beltrão seeks to build bridges between popular street dance and the more academic, indeed elitist world of theater. Through successive works, the young choreographer has reversed the virtuosity of street dance and freed hip-hop from its ghetto by making it the raw material of his own approach: repetitive movements and looped, stereotyped figures inspired by a macho, violent universe. In works such as *Too Legit to Quit* and *Me and My Choreographer in 63* Beltrão self-fictionalizes his persona on stage through a multiple series of solos. Yet every time, he adopts a certain distance from his subject. Although hip-hop is his scene of predilection, it sometimes seems as though he is ready to sabotage it.

His talent has been recently reconfirmed with works such as *H2* and *H3*. In the latter piece, the Brazilian choreographer displayed remarkable, original work that stuck close to the stage—this skill at floor work (or "ground knowledge," as he styles it) produced a show of raw energy that lasts less than an hour as ten performers constantly invent new dance figures based on movement-as-projection (two dancers launch a third) and work on sequences in reverse order, from back to front. Although his entire vocabulary stems from the original hip-hop, here it is dismantled in order to reveal a new grammar of the body. Beltrão conjugates dance in the future perfect.

Bruno Beltrão, *H3* (2008).

TRISHA BROWN

Trisha Brown, *Geometry of Quiet* (2002).

"**I make plays on movement like rhyming or echoing an earlier gesture in another part of the body at a later time and perhaps out of kilter. I turn phrases upside down, reverse them or suggest an action and then not complete it.**"

her background

Born in 1936, the American dancer and choreographer Trisha Brown had an academic training before studying various kinds of dance—from tap dancing to Martha Graham technique—at Mills College in California. She met Anna Halprin and then took classes at Merce Cunningham's studio. Brown was above all the instigator, along with a troupe of dancer-choreographers (Simone Forti, Yvonne Rainer, Steve Paxton) and musicians (Terry Riley and La Monte Young) of the Judson Dance Theater, named after a disaffected church in New York. Brown remains one of the leading figures of what was then called postmodern dance, which broke with a somewhat outdated idiom. In 1970 she founded her own company, which danced on rooftops and in galleries but wound up returning to more conventional venues in theaters and opera houses, where her projects have involved a merger of dance and opera.

her style

"Fluid" is one of the adjectives that recurs most frequently when describing Brown's dance style. Having laid the foundations for a new kind of dance with her friends at the Judson Church, Brown returned to the fold by founding a company with her own name and salaried members (which is not so common in the United States, where dancers often freelance from one job to the next, ranging from ballet to musical). Her renowned fluidity can nevertheless prickle with sharp angles and other destructurations. Right from the start, Brown has proceeded in cycles: "Equipment Pieces" with ropes and harnesses, "Accumulations" with their repeated movements, and "Unstable Molecular Structures" based on principles of improvisation. These somewhat ungainly categories in fact point to Brown's almost unceasing spirit of research. Not only does she sometimes seek analogy with mathematical structures, Brown also seeks human exchange, notably with artists such as painter Robert Rauschenberg and composer Laurie Anderson, who collaborated on one of her most successful pieces, *Set and Reset* (1983). Her dancers are given "instructions"—enter/exit, visible/invisible—and often move through a visual environment composed of photographs and pictures projected on a prism. The nature of the executed movements seems beholden simultaneously to chance and to a meticulously planned script. Finally, with her broad musical background Brown has also directed operas in which the role of dance was crucial. *Orfeo*, a hit production of 1998, had dancers literally fly across the stage. Having revived some of her early pieces at Documenta in Kassel and the Pompidou Center in Paris, Brown has enthusiastically begun work on *Pygmalion*, a baroque opera by Jean-Philippe Rameau. And a whole different world.

Trisha Brown, *It's a Draw* (2002).

BORIS CHARMATZ

his background

Chambéry, France, 1973, reads the birth certificate of Boris Charmatz, who would become an agitator on the French dance scene. Yet at first this young man in a hurry followed a classical career: dance school at the Paris Opera, followed by the Conservatoire National Supérieur de Musique et de Danse in Lyon. A sought-after dancer by some of the big names of 1980 choreography, such as Régine Chopinot (for *Ana* and *Saint-Georges*) and Odile Duboc (for *Projet de la matière* and *Trois boléros*), Charmatz nevertheless made a sharp change of direction in 1992 and founded the Edna association with his friend Dimitri Chamblas. *A bras-le-corps* (Bodily Seizure) was the duo's rebirth certificate. Ever since, Charmatz has followed a unique career as a kind of unfathomable body in the heavens of the current dance scene. A thinker and an original educator (in early 2000 he founded BOCAL, an itinerant, ephemeral school), an amazing dancer (notably his vision of the Faun and his jazz improvisations with Archie Shepp), and a leader of a company—Charmatz is all that. Today director of a revamped national choreographic center in Rennes called the Musée de la Danse, this veteran of European dance festival never fails to surprise.

his style

It is hard to fit Charmatz into a single style. In addition to his talent as a dancer with a strong classical background and extensive experience with contemporary choreographers, this angel-faced, eternal post-adolescent has composed several strong works. *A bras-le-corps*, his first duet, saw him in a magnified physical embrace full of power and contained sensuality. He then boldly devised a solo for dancer and sculpture, *Les Disparates* (Disparates); followed by a vertically inclined piece on three floors, *Aatt enen tionon* (1996); and a performance with artist Gilles Touyard, *Programme court avec essorage* (Short Cycle with Spin). As a sensitive intellectual, Charmatz investigates representations of the body—in *Con forts fleuve* the dancers wear jeans as hoods and half of the audience is dressed in black fabric. He also explores issues of audience perception—*Héâtre-élévision* (Heater-Elevision) is performed for one person at a time. More recently, Charmatz and actress Jeanne Balibar premiered *La danseuse malade* (The Unwell Ballerina), a frenzied project where dance, the visual arts, and performance art all intersect: the performers declaim fiery statements by Tatsumi Hijikata, the harbinger of Japanese Butoh, as they maneuver a small truck on stage or "blow up" their heads (an arty trick that divided critics). And yet once again Charmatz demonstrates a talent not so much for provocation as for catalyzing strong desires. Thus engaged, Charmatz occupies a special place in the landscape of French dance.

"Dance belongs to those who are not afraid to transform public spaces, that is to say, spaces of contagion and freedom for the truant desires of everyone." *

*Boris Charmatz, *Je suis une école*
(Paris: Les Prairies Ordinaires, 2009).

Boris Charmatz and Dimitri Chamblas, *À bras-le-corps* (Bodily Seizure, 1993).

SIDI LARBI CHERKAOUI

Sidi Larbi Cherkaoui, *Myth* (2007).

"There are so many things I want to learn. That's why I create so much. Sometimes I think I may not stay with dance all my life, even if I know that's where I enjoy the greatest freedom."

his background

Born in 1976 in Antwerp, to a Flemish mother and a Moroccan father, Sidi Larbi Cherkaoui is something of a boy wonder on the current dance scene. Following what seems to have been a lonely childhood, the separation of his parents gave Cherkaoui new impetus. He began in simple showbiz, as an extra in TV broadcasts and variety shows—whereas certain people might deny such a past, Cherkaoui draws strength from it. Once enrolled in P.A.R.T.S., the school founded by Anne Teresa De Keersmaeker, who revived Belgian dance in the 1980s, he discovered the existence of great choreographic innovators. But it was a contest for solo dance in Belgium, launched by Alain Platel in 1995, that accelerated Cherkaoui's transformation. As the contest winner, Cherkaoui participated in *Iets op Bach* (Something About Bach), a piece by Platel that was an international hit. On joining the Ballet C. de la B., Cherkaoui premiered *Rien de rien (Absolutely Nothing)*, which brought more kudos. He has subsequently worked with Akram Khan, the Ballet du Grand Théâtre in Geneva, and the Ballets de Monte-Carlo. On leaving the Ballets C de la B, he became artist-in-residence at the Tonelhuis in Antwerp.

his style

Cherkaoui has retained a taste for experimentation—and combination—from a varied dance career that spans disco, jazz, musicals, and contemporary dance. As a young man of his times, he constantly conflates everything, with one important proviso: as a perfectionist, he carries his ideas to the limit, even if it sometimes means heading down the wrong road. His first hit, *Rien de rien*, brought together on stage a teenager, a classical musician, a storyteller, and his former dance teacher; from that apparently disparate community Cherkaoui managed to produce a sensitive portrait. In subsequent shows, he has addressed the excesses of religion (*Foi* [Faith], 2003) and evil (*Myth*, 2007). As a member of the "Flemish school" of dance, he brings together dancers, circus people, actors, and singers in a single show. Such dialogue can create powerful images (a wolf-man, or a dance on sticks). At the same time, Cherkaoui fulfills an ever-growing number of commissions from neoclassical companies. In Geneva he produced *Loin* (Far), in which soloists express themselves in words and gestures; at Monte Carlo, he excelled in duets (*In Memoriam* and *Mea Culpa*). Song is an increasingly important part of his approach, and musicians often participate in the action. In *Zero Degrees*, Cherkaoui crossed swords with Akram Khan, another dancer with a hybrid background. In *Sutra* he brought Shaolin monks from China to participate in an exploration of their universe; as a vegetarian and a Buddhist sympathizer, Cherkaoui feels at home with the monks' practice of martial arts and meditation. Elsewhere, the ever-curious Cherkaoui has just produced a piece that is a tribute to Diaghilev's *Faun*—a clever insight from a child of this century.

Sidi Larbi Cherkaoui, *Foi* (Faith, 2003).

MARIE CHOUINARD

her background

Marie Chouinard, born in Quebec, Canada, in 1955, is yet another one of those children of classical ballet who packed up and moved to contemporary dance. For that matter, she headed abroad—Berlin and Bali. By 1979 she was choreographing her first solos, which marked her as a rising talent in Canada. *La petite danse sans nom* (Nameless Little Dance) generated controversy and was briefly banned, but established Chouinard's own style—organic, highly sexed dance. Her personal interest in tantric tradition and practice spurred her to choreograph *L'Amande et le diamant* (The Almond and the Diamond), representing the vulva and penis, respectively. From one work to another, Chouinard has explored the body of "the Other" with its outlines and shadowy areas; she favors liberated, blissful movement and refers to herself as "a receptacle for the world's vibrations."

her style

Chouinard's superb solos are a magnified, powerful staging of the nomadic female. The body is presented in poses not so much suggestive as dominating—the dancer is sovereign. In her ensemble pieces, such as *The Rite of Spring*, *Le cri du monde* (The Cry of the World), and *Orphée et Eurydice*, Chouinard tries to reinvent a tribe of dancers who lick and sniff one another on stage, performing lifts in an idiom borrowed from the animal world, presenting a series of tableaux sharply defined by the lighting. Chouinard has also tried her hand at more complicated choreographic constructions such as *bODY_rEMIX/les_vARIATIONS_gOLDBERG*, where performers were harnessed and supplied with crutches (indeed, artificial limbs) in a hindered dance that disturbed many members of the audience, some of whom may have preferred Chouinard's horned female figure in *L'après-midi d'un faune* (Afternoon of a Faun), produced in 1987. As a child, claims Chouinard, she was "marked by a documentary film on the dances of animals in rut." A highly individual way to return to one's roots—her dance is inscribed in the deepest recesses of her memory. Recently, in an event designed to raise money for her company, Chouinard made a personal investment in the form of a solo, *Gloires du matin* (Morning Glories), performed in her own studio in Montreal—hence in permanent residence.

"My source has always been the body itself ... especially the silence and breath, which make up the 'invisible' stuff of life."

Marie Chouinard, *The Rite of Spring* (1993), Mathilde Monnard and Dominique Porte.

MERCE CUNNINGHAM

Merce Cunningham, *Split Sides* (2003),
Daniel Squire and Holley Farmer.

his background

Born in Centralia, Washington, in 1919, Merce Cunningham first studied theater and then dance at the Cornish Institute of Applied Arts in Seattle. He trained under Bonnie Bird, and struck up a relationship with the pianist who accompanied her classes, namely the composer John Cage. Cunningham went on to a career as a virtuoso dancer; noticed by Martha Graham, he danced with her company from 1939 to 1945. But by 1943 he was making forays into choreography, and in 1953 he founded his own company at Black Mountain College, with Cage as artistic director. Their partnership would last until Cage's death in 1992. Cunningham nevertheless surrounded himself with other artists—visual, musical, and video. Above all, he made a radical break with ballet and also, to a certain extent, with modern dance. His early efforts sparked both curiosity and incomprehension, resulting in a difficult start. But in 1964 he toured Europe for the first time, where he performed in France and Austria, presenting an *Event*, namely a piece for a specific site, often outside a theater, composed of excerpts from his repertoire. The Cunningham signature of abstraction, poetry, and virtuosity subsequently won worldwide recognition.

his style

Did Merce Cunningham invent everything in and for contemporary dance? Obviously not—but more than anyone else, he experimented. He subverted the point of view imposed by classical ballet by choreographing not around the center of the stage but around the dancer him- or herself, who thus became their own centers. With Cage he pioneered the use of chance in dance, while with Charles Atlas and Elliot Caplan he pioneered the use of video. Finally, in the 1990s Cunningham explored computer-aided choreography in order to venture into a new choreographic realms; he would compose with the software, then rework things in the studio to elaborate new trajectories. Above all a man of abstraction at the expense of narrative, he altered the beholder's point of view, working on a multiplicity of scenic propositions, rejecting frontality. The spinal column served as the axis of his choreographed movement, revealing dancers with torso and limbs thrust forward like birds with distinct grace, as witnessed by the title of one of his best-known pieces, *Beach Birds*. Calling upon contemporary artists, he "commissioned" sets from Robert Rauschenberg, Jasper Johns, and Andy Warhol. He favored live, contemporary music, and in addition to collaborators such as Cage and Takehisa Kosugi, he invited Radiohead, Sigur Rós, and Sonic Youth to compose dance music. But he never abandoned his principle of creating music and choreography entirely separately. The only thing the two shared was the same duration. As the author of nearly two hundred works, Cunningham influenced successive generations of dancers and choreographers through his technique and his dance studio as well as his company. In the spring of 2009, as he approached ninety, he premiered a work of infectious vitality titled *Nearly Ninety*. It was a hymn to life. Cunningham died on July 26th of that year.

"**Movement by itself is what absolutely touches me. Not when the movement describes something, but when the movement itself has a life.**"

Merce Cunningham, *Way Station* (2001), Cédric Andrieux and Derry Swan.

PHILIPPE DECOUFLÉ

Philippe Decouflé, *Sombrero* (2007).

**"I feed off my 'dancers,'
something that hasn't changed
since I started. Indeed I like
the idea that my creativity
is expressed through someone
else's body."**

his background

Born in 1961, as a teenager Philippe Decouflé took a summer course in physical expression given by I. Alvarez. He also studied circus techniques at the École Nationale du Cirque and mime techniques at Marcel Marceau's school, then headed toward dance via a stint at the Centre National de Danse Contemporaine in Angers at a time when Alwin Nikolais was director of the center. As a great stylistic inventor, Nikolais profoundly influenced Decouflé who, still only eighteen years old, was invited to join the master's company. It was a golden opportunity for an imaginative boy enamored of graphic novels. Decouflé also took courses with Merce Cunningham, yet failed to gain entry to Maurice Béjart's school, Mudra. Prior to choreographing his own pieces (*Vague Café*), he danced with Régine Chopinot and Karole Armitage. His first major success was *Codex* in 1986. He has been startling audiences ever since.

his style

To a certain extent, Decouflé's trademark is easily recognizable: a skillful blend of humor, visual effects, and truly offbeat choreography. This combination has made him one of the most popular choreographers of recent decades. In *Codex*, an explosion of creativity triggered by a codex, or scholarly book, the dance seems to leaf through a volume of pictures each more outrageous than the last. Everything seems to make sense in this universe of life-size microbes, from a gentle giant of a protagonist (actor Christophe Salengro wearing flippers) to machine-like dancers. As his career progressed, Decouflé refined his obsessions, playing with shadows (*Sombrero*), with gravity (*Shazam!*) and exoticness (*Le Japon dans l'iris* [Japan in the Iris]). He combines music (sometimes performed live), movies, and dark humor in the manner of a graphic novelist. He defines himself not as a full-time choreographer but rather as an artistic director who marshals the energies of his troupe, which has included future choreographers (Herman Diephuis and Jérôme Bel, among others). Above all, by agreeing to participate in Jean-Paul Goude's parade to celebrate the bicentenary of the French Revolution in 1989, Decouflé joined the privileged circle of star entertainers, as confirmed by his organization of the opening and closing ceremonies of the 1992 Winter Olympic Games. He subsequently refused several lucrative offers, although he produced a show for the Cirque du Soleil and assumed the artistic direction of the famous nude revue in Paris, the Crazy Horse. In 2004 Decouflé returned to basics—dance—with a rather moving solo portrait, *Le doute m'habite* (Haunted by Doubts), in which he shared the stage with himself in the form of shadows and projected images. Decouflé is willing to let dance sow its wild oats.

Philippe Decouflé, *Solo* (2003).

ANNE TERESA DE KEERSMAEKER

Anne Teresa De Keersmaeker, *D'un soir un jour*
(A Day in a Night, 2006).

"I have always maintained close links with nature, maybe because at heart I am, despite everything, romantic. As a child I liked to work on the farm and in the field. My love of tall mountains came later, when I began to hike.... I am unable to think at a desk, I need a trajectory and movement."

her background

A leading figure on the Belgian dance scene, Anne Teresa De Keersmaeker was born in Malines in 1960. After early classes in classical ballet, she left to enroll in Maurice Béjart's school in Brussels, Mudra (where she notably studied rhythm with Fernand Schirren from 1978 to 1980), then went on to the Tisch School of the Arts in New York. In 1982 she took the first step toward international recognition with *Fase*, a piece choreographed to music by Steve Reich; this duet (partnered by Michèle-Anne de Mey) was an amazing series of repetitive figures. De Keersmaeker very quickly established her own style as a dancer-choreographer—lots of female energy, white socks and little boots, a skirt and blouse—which was expressed through her own company, Rosas. What is most striking about De Keersmaeker's work, in addition to the radical choreographic idiom and all the running around, is her musicality. She even went so far as to devise dance-concerts, boldly exploring all possibilities—jazz, classical, Indian ragas, contemporary music. After years in residence at the Brussels opera house, she recovered an independent existence; in 1995, she founded a school, P.A.R.T.S., whose reputation continues to grow.

her style

De Keersmaeker long worked with and for female dancers, perhaps less from a feminist perspective than from a desire to know herself—her selves—better. This produced, during the first decade of her career, a sardonic virtuosity mixed with a desire to show people a thing or two, often based on tensions, accelerations, and falls. Open to various realms of music, De Keersmaeker has explored opera (*Ottone, Ottone*) and, more recently, the music of John Coltrane (*A Love Supreme*) and Miles Davis (*Bitches Brew–Tacoma Narrow*). Acquiring a certain sense of theatricality, the Flemish choreographer has partly reinvigorated her dance scores, but she remains most convincing when she returns to raw movement, as witnessed by successes such as *Rain*, *April Me*, and *Drumming*. *The Song* (2009) is a pared-down piece almost devoid of music, relying instead on live sound effects, pointing toward a new and fascinating direction. More than once De Keersmaeker has "retraced her steps," that is to say revived works such as *Fase* and *Rosas Danst Rosas*—with good reason, given the richness of her repertoire. De Keersmaeker, with her intense character, is today recognized as one of the major choreographic artists of her day.

Anne Teresa De Keersmaeker, *D'un soir un jour* (A Day in a Night, 2006)

MATS EK

Mats Ek, *Carmen* (1992), Anna Laguna.

his background

Born in Malmö, Sweden, in 1945, Mats Ek was a theater brat. His mother, Birgit Cullberg, joined German choreographer Kurt Jooss in England when he was driven out by the Nazis, then she returned to Sweden after the war and revolutionized the dance scene there. Ek's father, Anders Ek, was a star of stage and screen, as well as a fan of psychoanalysis; he also took dance lessons. Mats Ek first studied theater, and then dance with Donya Feuer. He became a director at the Marionette Theater in Stockholm and was twenty-seven years old before he performed with the Cullberg Ballet. He subsequently became a high-profile choreographer and finally artistic director of the company (from 1980 to 1993). Right from his early ballets, Ek, as a "citizen of the world," dealt with political themes such as apartheid and imperialism. He won an international reputation with his biting reinterpretations of classics such as *The House of Bernarda Alba* (1978), *Giselle* (1984), and *Swan Lake* (1987). His pieces have entered the repertoire of the greatest companies, making Ek, who also continues to work in the legitimate theater, the jewel in the crown of Scandinavian dance.

his style

Ek's signature style, which he developed from one ballet to another, is based on a dense vocabulary: sudden if sometimes rounded movements of the arms, energetic leaps, floor work. In his reinterpretations of classics (from *Giselle* to *Sleeping Beauty*) people butt their heads like animals and slide beneath their partners for strange, amorous displays. Everything is done with a concern for realism, eschewing the silly side of classical ballet with its eternal fairy tales. Thus Ek's Giselle is not dispatched to the kingdom of the shades but rather to an insane asylum, while his Sleeping Beauty looks like an unhappy drug addict. Everyday incidents—the little nothings of daily life as well as grand love affairs—are also a source of endless inspiration to Ek, who admits that when he dances he always tries to express something. In one of his latest works, *The Place*, he brought together on stage Mikhail Baryshnikov, the greatest dancer of the 1970s and 1980s, and his wife Anna Laguna; the piece recounts their joint "life," the torments of a couple that has undergone many trials, affair after affair. This duet of rare intensity goes straight to the heart. Baryshnikov has heaped praise on Ek, and hopes to work with him again.

Ek is probably the finest example of a dancer who managed to inject his original "classicism" into a contemporary world accessible to all. Which takes real talent.

"Movement is a language. It's not aesthetic or decorative, nor is it just an illustration of music. It's a form of expression."

Mats Ek, *Giselle* (1984), Marie-Agnès Gillot, prima ballerina with the Paris Opera Ballet

JAN FABRE

Jan Fabre, *Swan Lake* (2002), Royal Ballet of Flanders.

his background

Born in Antwerp, in 1958, Jan Fabre trained first as a visual artist, having studied at the local institute of decorative and applied arts, and then at the Academy of Fine Arts in Antwerp. Drawn toward performance art—in *Money Performances* he burned banknotes in order to create works from their ashes—he drew pictures with his own blood or with a blue ballpoint pen. In 1980, aged twenty-two, he tried his hand at the theater with *Théâtre écrit avec un K est un matou* (Theater Spelled with a K is a Cat), and soon attracted attention with *Le Pouvoir des folies théâtrales* (The Power of Theatrical Follies), an action divided into ninety-six vignettes set against a backdrop of mannerist paintings. Fabre also dabbled in the movies but ultimately won recognition in the realm of dance with *Das Glas im Kopf wird vom Glas–Dance Sections* (Glass in the Head Will be Made of Glass), an opera with a corps de ballet. Fabre wrote and worked with the Royal Ballet of Flanders on a reinterpretation of *Swan Lake*, he went back and forth between installations and choreography (both solo and ensemble pieces), and never seemed to want to restrict himself to a single style. He was invited to produce a piece at the Avignon Theater Festival in 2005, a more than controversial affair. He has also had a solo exhibition of his work in the galleries of the Louvre Museum in Paris.

his style

Having had no training in dance strictly speaking (much less in choreography), Fabre relies essentially on the presence of his performers, whom he usually chooses with great intelligence. He has worked in a "grand ballet" mode—both classical and modern—and also in a "broad fresco" approach with a soft spot for his trademark "warriors of beauty" (dancers dressed in armor and scanty underwear). His powerful visual universe remains very coherent from one work to another, and is characterized by nudity, rawness, and skillfully composed tableaus. Little by little Fabre has begun adopting overtly critical themes (religion, consumerism, etc.). In *Orgie de la tolérance* (Orgy of Tolerance), he brought together on stage ersatz extremists (the Ku Klux Klan), fans of contemporary fashion, and hard rockers, creating an exaggerated, global farce that sometimes hit home. Perhaps more successful and accomplished are solos such as *Body, Body on the Wall* (in which dancer-choreographer Wim Vandekeybus is daubed in paint) and *The Fin Comes a Little Bit Earlier this Siècle* (in which Icelandic performer Erna Omarsdottir plays with a lump of butter), not forgetting *Another Sleepy Dusty Delta Day* (featuring Fabre's partner, Ivana Jozic) and *Quando l'Uomo principale è una donna* (When the Principal Man is a Woman, where the ballerina dances nude in swirls of olive oil). Fabre perpetuates a Flemish tradition in which the grotesque and the beautiful are one and the same.

"The theater should be the site of a chemical transformation of the actor's body."

Jan Fabre, *L'Histoire des larmes* (The History of Tears, 2005).

WILLIAM FORSYTHE

William Forsythe, *In the Middle, Somewhat Elevated*
(1987), Ballets de Monte-Carlo.

"Ballet has never been retro.
It is in my body and I live with it.
It is very contemporary and you
can't just erase it ... you can't
erase it from your consciousness."

his background

William Forsythe, born in 1949, was crazy about musicals as a kid, but "went straight," so to speak, once he joined the Joffrey Ballet after studying ballet and jazz dance at Jacksonville University. In 1973 he suddenly struck out in a new direction, accepting a position at the prestigious Stuttgart Ballet, a neoclassical company in Germany. There he met John Cranko and Marica Haydée. A new stage in his career came in 1984 with his appointment as artistic director of the Frankfurt Ballet. Forsythe transformed that dull institution into the most intrepid neoclassical ballet company of the century. His dazzling reinterpretation of the classical vocabulary and the intelligence of his staging made Forsythe a leading figure. His ballets were appreciated by classical ballet fans and the contemporary crowd alike, thereby effecting the unanticipated reconciliation of the two genres. The greatest companies in the world—including the Paris Opera Ballet, the San Francisco Ballet, and the New York City Ballet—have commissioned works from him. In 2000, following pressure from Frankfurt's municipal institutions, he closed down the large, unwieldy company and then founded his own troupe, The Forsythe Company, with a more modest personnel of twenty dancers. Forsythe divides his time between Frankfurt and Dresden—when he is not trotting around the rest of the globe.

his style

As implied above, there have been several "lives" to Forsythe's artistic career, and therefore several styles. In the 1980s he proposed a classical universe, simultaneously baroque and deconstructed, composed of large works that ran the gamut of the classical idiom—pas de deux, leaps, lifts—in order to push the limits ever further. From *Artifact* (1984) to *Impressing the Czar* (1988), a deluge of dance poses, sometimes on toes, seemed to redraw the ballerina's silhouette: legs rose higher, arms etched the theatrical horizon, and—above all—hips and pelvis henceforth adopted sharp angles, thrust forward or to the side. The virtuosity of these choreographed bodies served as the bridge between past and future. Some of Forsythe's major works are still in the repertoire of bolder companies such as the Royal Ballet of Flanders and the Lyon Opera Ballet. In the years between 1990 and 2000, meanwhile, the choreographer ventured into frankly contemporary waters, in which texts made a notable appearance, to the extent of upsetting part of his audience. The public was notably struck by *One Flat Thing Reproduced* (a ballet in which the stage is cluttered with tables) and *Three Atmospheric Studies* (a triptych against a backdrop of war in the Middle East). The dancers worked tirelessly at pulling off bold experiments, whether upright or on the floor.

In recent years Forsythe has changed direction once again, as exemplified by "performance choreographies" such as *Heterotopia*, in which the audience is invited to wander between two stages—two worlds—as do the dancers. A new choreographic vocabulary and idiom is thereby invented "live." Forsythe once forged the slogan, "Welcome to what you think you see." It still holds.

William Forsythe, *One Flat Thing Reproduced* (2000), Lyon Opera Ballet.

ISRAEL GALVÁN

Israel Galván, *Arena* (2004).

"I don't try to experiment at all costs. When I feel good while dancing, it's because I'm beyond all risk."

his background

Born in Seville, Spain, in 1973 to a pair of well-known dancers, Eugenia de los Reyes and José Galván, Israel Galván accompanied his father to dance academies and fiestas from the age of five. Such precociousness is not all that rare in the world of flamenco. Aged seventeen, Israel finally decided to devote himself body and soul to dance. In 1994 he joined Mario Maya's Compania Andaluza de Danza. Soon Galván was winning prestigious prizes. His path also crossed those of some great names in flamenco, such as Manuel Soler and Manuela Carasco, not forgetting vocalist Vicente Amigo. In 1998, Galván finally moved from dance into choreography with *¡Mira! Los Zapatos Rojos*, in collaboration with his associate, the director Pedro G. Romero. Above all, Galván broke with the flamenco recital format—whether purist or neo-contemporary—by adding a dose of theatricality to his shows. Kafka made an appearance in *Metamorphosis*, while bulls were celebrated as the main theme of *Arena*. Since then, Galván's reputation has largely outgrown the small circle of insiders. Some people have compared him to Nijinsky, and he is invited to today's dance festivals in cities such as Montpellier, Marseille, and Avignon.

his style

As strange as it may seem, Galván is considered here to be a contemporary choreographer. Obviously, he hasn't renounced his roots in flamenco, that extended, boisterous family to which he pays tribute in *La edad de oro* (The Golden Age), his finest work. But his approach reflects the influence, whether acknowledged or not, of classical ballet, Butoh (the Japanese "dance of darkness"), rock music, and the movies. A wonderful dancer, usually standing in profile, Galván reconciles the purists with all the others through his grace and his passion. In a recent work, *El final de este estado de cosas, redux* (The End of this State of Things, Redux), he shares the stage with flamenco and rock musicians, himself thumping on a drum or a coffin, appearing bare-chested with a mask over his face. He blithely dances on a floating podium that rollicks as though the earth were staggering beneath his "blows." *Arena* is another piece of bravura, with its dreadful images of a bullfight crowd as Galván plays with a rocking chair, which provides further proof of its author's uniqueness. He alternates small pieces with large works without ever striving for a whole "show," unlike his compatriots Maria Pagès and Sara Baras. Above all, Galván draws an audience new to the highly codified—and, to many people, impenetrable—world of flamenco. As a child he wanted to be a soccer star; today he is becoming a performance star. One who constantly amazes, and will continue to do so.

Israel Galván, *El final de este estado de cosas, redux* (The End of this State of Things, Redux, 2009).

RAIMUND HOGHE

Raimund Hoghe, *36, Avenue Georges-Mandel* (2008).

"It is important to see non-standard bodies on stage, not only from a historical standpoint but also from the standpoint of current developments that tend to reduce the status of people to that of artifacts or design items."

his background

Raimund Hoghe was born in 1949 in Wuppertal, Germany, a city made famous by Pina Bausch, who was based there until she died. He started out as a writer and reporter, notably for *Die Zeit* newspaper, becoming a "specialist" in portraits of people both unknown and famous. But his life suddenly changed when he became the dramatist for—who else?—Pina Bausch. Over a ten-year period, from 1980 to 1990, he worked with the grand dame of the Wuppertal Tanztheater, who had been one of the first choreographers to give her dancers spoken lines. Hoghe's contributions to key Bausch works such as *1980, Bandoneon, Nelken,* and *Viktor* were magnificent. As this venture came to an end, Hoghe took up his pen again to write solos for, among other people, former members of the Wuppertal Tanztheater (*Verdi Prati,* 1992, and *Geraldo's Solo,* 1996). Above all, Hoghe himself appeared on stage with his unconventional physique—his spine is deformed, leaving him with a hunchback since birth—in the 1994 *Meinwarts,* in which he referred, in his sensitive way, to friends carried off by AIDS. It was the first part of a trilogy on the twentieth century. As a performer fond of classicism and old, sentimental songs, Hoghe said—quoting Pasolini—that he felt he had to "throw [his] body into the battle."

his style

As one work follows another—halfway between theater and dance—Hoghe has been etching an intaglio portrait of himself even as he develops a distinct style. Fortunately, Hoghe does not simply rehash Bausch. His solos, as well as some of his ensemble pieces, seem closer to the process of danced ritual: in *Young People, Old Voices* (2002), which won him an even wider reputation, he places himself on the side of young people who seem to relive, on stage, the amorous emotions, desire, and banality of that difficult age. Little happens, and yet everything seems to move, whether a lively diagonal thrust or a game played by two. Hoghe's version of *The Rite of Spring* is unsettling: he confronts a young boy, Lorenzo de Brabandere, in a vaguely erotic one-on-one. He also produced a very personal version of *Swan Lake, Four Acts,* with a real classical ballerina, Ornella Balestra. Hoghe summons up a world specific to popular culture, such as songs by Dalida or Maria Callas, or Ravel's *Boléro.* The subtlety at work in Hoghe's oeuvre today makes him one of the key—if indirect—influences on choreographers such as Boris Charmatz (who staged Hoghe in one of his own works) and Jérôme Bel.

Raimund Hoghe, *36, Avenue Georges-Mandel* (2008).

GILLES JOBIN

Gilles Jobin, *Steak House* (2005).

his background

Gilles Jobin, born in Switzerland in 1964, grew up in an artistic environment—his father, Arthur Jobin, was known for his abstract painting. Gilles
studied classical ballet at Rosella Hightower's school in Cannes, then
danced with Swiss companies. He was named co-director of a venue in
Geneva known for its contemporary creativity, the Théâtre de l'Usine, but
it was in Madrid, Spain, that Jobin came to international attention with
his trilogy *Bloody Mary, Middle Suisse,* and *Only You.* He then moved to a
new base, London, where he refined his compositional style in conjunction with his partner, the dancer-choreographer Maria La Ribot; the pair
founded a company called Parano Productions, revealing a distinct humor.
With each new work, from *A+B = X* to *Text to Speech,* Jobin explored territory new to dance by incorporating electronic music and video art.

his style

What is striking—and delightful—about Jobin is his willingness to place
himself in danger with each new production in order to explore more
deeply the raw material of dance: the performer's body. His sense of composition—among the most accomplished of his generation—targets
abstraction in an effort to avoid the pitfalls of storytelling, yet he has a
way of developing a theme and fully exploring it. This can been seen, for
example, in the floor work of soloists in *Two-Thousand-and-Three* (commissioned by the Ballet du Grand Théâtre in Geneva) who crawl on the
ground before merging into a maelstrom of bodies, and in the duet-like
sequences in *Double Deux,* in which the dancers drive one another in an
hour-long series of dazzlingly beautiful movements ranging from dramatic
falls to kisses via a rather fun "waltz." One of the special features of Jobin's
oeuvre is his openness to formal experiment and other musical and visual
variables: in *Steak House* the company built and dismantled the walls of
an imaginary world based on the covers of 45-rpm records. The widely
hailed *Moebius Strip* (2001), meanwhile, exploited motifs such as a grid-
ded set to reveal a three-dimensional choreographic construction. Finally,
in *Text to Speech* Jobin investigated an almost documentary kind of dance,
featuring screens on stage—some members of the audience, however,
did not get caught up in this fool's game. One of Jobin's more recent works,
Black Swan, represented a return to a simple quartet, "a gentle dance
nourished on the feelings of the one who embodies it," according to Jobin.
A wonderful, far-reaching concept if ever there were one.

**"Avoid the predictable in both
the vocabulary of dance and
the structures of composition."**

Gilles Jobin, *Two-Thousand-And-Three* (2003), Ballet du Grand Théâtre de Genève.

AKRAM KHAN

Akram Khan, *Kaash* (2003).

his background

Born in London in 1974 to Bangladeshi parents, Akram Khan was only thirteen when he first went on stage, cast in the role of Ekalavya in Peter Brook's celebrated production of the *Mahabharata*. After studying at De Montfort University and the Northern School of Contemporary Dance in Leeds, Khan attended P.A.R.T.S., the multidisciplinary school run by Belgian choreographer Anne Teresa De Keersmaeker. In 2000, he founded his own company. Two solos, *Polaroid Feet* and *Ronin*, were notably followed by *Kaash* (2002), a work produced in collaboration with famous sculptor Anish Kapoor, opening wide the door to success. In subsequent productions, Khan developed this taste for working with others, notably dancers such as Sidi Larbi Cherkaoui (*Zero Degrees*) and Sylvie Guillem (*Sacred Monsters*), writers such as Hanif Kureishi, musicians such as Nitin Sawhney, and movie stars such as Juliette Binoche (who danced for the first time in Khan's *In-I*).

his style

To a certain extent, there are two Khans, and therefore two styles. The first is a dancer of kathak, a traditional, centuries-old form of dance from northern India characterized by driving rhythms and rapid footwork with jangling anklets. Khan not only gives kathak recitals, but sometimes playfully introduces a taste of it in more ambitious pieces such as *Sacred Monsters*, featuring the *ballerina assoluta* Sylvie Guillem. The other, contemporary, Khan likes precise, virtuoso dance that accords with the changing environments and moods of the choreographer. In particular Khan likes building bridges between East and West, pointing out mutual misunderstandings in a constantly evolving world. In one of his latest works, *Bahok*, he brought together classically trained dancers with contemporary performers in order to engineer a fusion of bodies. His dance, with its repetitive movements, is like a seismograph of the times, yet makes no accusations. Indeed, his choreography can be unsettlingly sweet, as one dancer falls asleep on the shoulder of another in the midst of a series of sophisticated falls. What audiences most recall about *Zero Degrees* is the artificial ball game played with Sidi Larbi Cherkaoui's head in Khan's hands. Sometimes his dancers also deliver spoken lines in works that imagine other possible worlds. The highly gifted Khan continues to surprise audiences through his reconciliation of tradition and avant-garde.

"We are all travelers. We are all voyagers."

Akram Khan, *Zero Degrees* (2005).

SUSANNE LINKE

Susanne Linke, *Märkische Landschaft* (1996).

her background

The daughter of a pastor, born in Germany in 1944, Susanne Linke first studied under Mary Wigman in Berlin, then headed to Essen where she enrolled in the famous Folkwang school originally founded by Kurt Jooss but at that time run by Pina Bausch. Her career then took her to the Rotterdam Dans Centrum. Linke's earliest choreography dates from the 1970s (*Danse funèbre,* 1975, and *Trop tard* [Too Late], 1977, were particularly noted in France). She wound up becoming the director of the Folkwang Tanz Studio, first jointly with Reinhild Hoffmann, then on her own. She combined her personal pieces with group work and experimentation. In 1985 she reclaimed her independence, producing a tribute to Dore Hoyer (a major figure of German dance) and accepting invitations from the Nederlands Dans Theater and the Groupe de Recherche Chorégraphique at the Paris Opera. She then founded the Susanne Linke Company in 1990, all the while actively participating in the Bremer Tanztheater and the Essen Choreographic Center. Although perhaps overshadowed by Pina Bausch's aura, Linke has nevertheless been a key figure in the revival of German—and international—dance. The interest in her work shown by the likes of Jérôme Bel—who went so far as to dance like her in his *Dernier spectacle* (Last Show), proclaiming all the while, "Ich bin Susanne Linke"—underscore her unique contribution.

her style

Her training made Linke an heir to Tanztheater yet also an inventor of new forms. A certain quality of movement infused with derision assumed full importance in her many solos, which are often produced as responses to a group piece. Thus the solo *Im Bade Wannen* (Bath Tubbing), whose main prop is a bathtub, alludes to the 1980 ballet *Wowerwiewas.* A markedly female choreographer, Linke nevertheless explored male violence in *Ruhr-Ort* whose subtle staging evoked the steel factories in that industrial region of Germany. In *Le coq est mort* (The Rooster is Dead) she drifted toward Africa with members of Germaine Acogny's Ballet Jant-Bi. In 2005 the Paris Opera Ballet commissioned *Ich Bin...* (I Am...), a patient piece of choreographic archaeology in which Linke explored a solo by Mary Wigman for which there survived only a few photos—her daring choreography was thus perched between memory and future. Magnificently.

In 2008 Linke surprised audiences once again with a reinterpretation of *Schritte Verfolgen II,* a solo that she expanded for four dancers, including herself. The title could be translated as "retracing your steps," and alludes to Linke's own childhood: as a result of meningitis, she could neither speak nor hear until the age of six. Since then, however, she has certainly learned how to express herself.

"I never begin unless I have a theme, an emotion, a feeling. For me, emotion comes first, movement follows."

Susanne Linke, *Ruhr-Ort* (1991).

RUSSELL MALIPHANT

Russell Maliphant, *Small Boats* (2007).

"**I'll use any vocabulary that's appropriate at the time ... I'm as interested in the uplift of ballet as I am in the gravity of modern dance.**"

his background

Although born in Ottawa, Canada, in 1961, Russell Maliphant trained at the very classical Royal Ballet in London. The slender dancer first performed with the Sadler's Wells Royal Ballet, then with companies headed by Lloyd Newson (DV8 Physical Theater) and Michael Clark, that is to say the cream of British dance. Maliphant founded his own company in 1996. As a practitioner of both tai chi (originally from China) and yoga (from India), Maliphant is clearly a man of dialogue. The people he has worked with include star ballerina Sylvie Guillem, with whom he shared the limelight in *Eonnagata*, staged by the Canadian director Robert Lepage. Maliphant has also collaborated with British video artist Isaac Julien.

his style

With Maliphant, everything is harmonious—his choreographic compositions favor curves over sharp edges. Thanks to a thorough training that ranges from classical ballet and contemporary dance to capoeira (a Brazilian martial art) and Asian physical arts, Maliphant is constantly attuned to new approaches. In *Flux*, a solo inspired by one of his favorite dancers, Alexander Varona, Maliphant daringly brought the performer to his knees—and then had him dance. The movement is constantly drawn out, as though the choreographer wanted to shatter the standard framework. In *Broken Fall*, a trio composed for Sylvie Guillem (a *ballerina assoluta* on the rebound from classical roles), William Trevitt, and Michael Nunn, Maliphant invented a new language based on the figure of a pas de trois: the audience had to observe keenly to know who began a movement, who ended it, to whom this arm or that leg belonged. The key idea at work here, which Maliphant has been developing from one piece to another, is indeed the flow, or flux, that unites performers on stage. In this respect, the duet *Push* is probably Maliphant's most successful work thanks to the constant exchange between a man and a woman caught in their choreographic élan. Between lifts and twists, the idiom employed here transcends the usual division between classic, modern, and contemporary. Maliphant himself likes to say that he doesn't want to restrict himself to a single style. He compares his vision of movement to the gaze of a sculptor. His dance is soothing, like a balm.

Russell Maliphant, *Small Boats* (2007).

MAGUY MARIN

Maguy Marin, *Turba* (2007).

her background

Of Spanish stock, Maguy Marin was born in Toulouse, France, in 1951. She studied at the conservatory then began her career with the very classical Strasbourg Opera. The break came when she went to Brussels and enrolled in Mudra, the multidisciplinary school run by Maurice Béjart. For four years she was a soloist with Béjart's Ballet of the 20th Century, before joining the new wave of auteur-choreographers who flooded the French dance scene in the late 1980s. By founding the Ballet Théâtre de l'Arche in conjunction with Daniel Ambasch, Marin laid the foundation stone of an institution that continues to rule the stage; renamed the Compagnie Maguy Marin when located near Paris, the troupe is based today in Rillieux-la-Pape near Lyon,

her style

Marin's multiple centers of interest make it essential to refer to her styles in the plural. Not because she is still seeking her own style, but simply because the scope of her choreographic activity transcends any single category. This diversity has made Marin a uniquely strong innovator on the French—and foreign—scene. After a few warm-up pieces with pleasant titles like *Evocation* and *Nieblas de niño* (The Fog of Childhood), she moved into higher gear in 1981 with *May B*. Inspired by the world of Samuel Beckett, first performed during a time of political change in France, this show caught imaginations and unsettled audiences: on stage was a mass of humanity with bodies of indefinite shape and faces smeared with chalky white makeup; the piece was an epic of a world undergoing transformation. As her oeuvre developed, Marin's highly theatrical dance challenged certainties even as it interrogated both sexuality and religion. At the request of the Lyon Opera Ballet, Marin also attacked the classics, giving them new life. Her 1995 *Cinderella* included masked dancers with grotesque features, and her 1993 *Coppelia* was set in a housing project and used projected imagery. Both ballets, in which choreographic movement was fluid and the drama was simplified, were triumphs. *Waterzooi* and, more recently, *Umwelt* (Environment) and *Turba* are examples of shows somewhere between performance art, theater, and dance: a kind of total artwork of rare visual power. *Description d'un combat*, presented at the 2009 Avignon Theater Festival, provided new proof of Marin's political and artistic commitment: working with her "twin," the composer Denis Mariotte, Marin spun and then wove "the ties that bind" so tightly that audiences were startled once again. Many people feel that Marin has found her rightful place in the world of dance—at the summit.

"Art constantly works toward the perception of a stunning reality that daily life hides from us, making us overlook it."

Maguy Marin, *Umwelt* (Environment, 2004).

MOURAD MERZOUKI

his background

Born in Lyon, France, to Algerian parents in 1973, Mourad Merzouki began his career as a performing artist in the martial arts and the circus. Aged fifteen, he shifted into urban dance, namely hip-hop, a form that he has enriched ever since. Open to the world of contemporary choreography (having frequented the likes of Josef Nadj and Maryse Delent), in 1989 Merzouki founded his first company, Accrorap, in conjunction with the similarly talented Kader Attou. His first success came with *Athina*, performed at the Biennial Dance Festival in Lyon, an institution that has become a faithful supporter of his. In 1996 Merzouki launched a new troupe, Kâfig ("Cage" in Arabic), which was followed by worldwide tours and well-received new works. He has also contributed to theatrical plays directed by Claudia Stavisky, imparting movement to words. Initially based in Bron (near Lyon), Merzouki and his company now run the Centre Chorégraphique National in Creteil, just outside Paris.

Mourad Merzouki, *Agwa* (Water, 2008).

his style

Merzouki is clearly a "product of the street" in so far as that is where he draws his contagious—and sometimes outrageous—energy. Given his background in circus, hip-hop, and contemporary dance, this auteur-choreographer has granted letters of nobility to urban dance, opening wide his own horizons. In a work such as *Terrain vague* (Vacant Lot), he recalls the wandering days of his childhood, trapped between hope and rejection. He turns a fence into a trampoline for soaring figures, or turns a lamppost into a dance partner to be braved. He of course calls upon familiar moves—such as the head spin, arm spin, and glide—but his appetite for openness eludes the standard pitfalls. His choreography is hip-hop, but not *only* hip-hop. He brings on stage contortionist clowns and human pyramids that defy the laws of gravity. From *Kâfig* to *Récital*, this full-fledged choreographer has been redefining the stakes behind urban dance, urging it to grow up. In *Agwa*, a Franco-Brazilian project, Merzouki called upon dancers from Rio de Janeiro—a hive of hip-hop—to perform an amazingly ingenious ballet. The sole props, plastic cups, symbolize water (the *agwa* of the title), and are employed by the soloists as both constraint and asset as they dance among and with these props. This apt, ecologically aware and moving piece proves that hip-hop truly merits its place in dance theaters. And Merzouki's talent no longer needs worry about smashing walls.

"One goal: to rid myself of clichés and preconceptions, free myself from commonplaces such as 'socially aware hip-hop' in order to build this language into an autonomous mode of artistic expression."

Mourad Merzouki, *Terrain vague* (Vacant Lot, 2006).

MATHILDE MONNIER her background

Mathilde Monnier's initials echo the "M" of Mulhouse, were she was born in 1956, and Montpellier, where she is currently based. As a dancer and choreographer who studied under Viola Farber at the Centre National de la Danse Contemporaine in Angers, then came to notice in the mid-1980s, Monnier paved a path of all-out experimentation—initially with Jean-François Duroure, later on her own—on behalf of an entire generation of artists. Her first, highly danced works were delightful in their fully assumed femininity and their work on movement as an extension of the body. From 1986 to 1988, *Pudique acide* (Modest Acid), *Mort de rire* (Helpless Laughter), and *Je ne vois pas la femme cachée dans la forêt* (I Can't See the Woman Hiding in the Forest) were premiered to great effect. But soon Monnier was leaving the beaten track, collaborating with a jazz musician, Louis Sclavis, on *Chinoiserie*, or traveling to Burkino Faso where she invited dancers to come to France to work with her (Salia Sanou and Seydou Boro have since become leading figures in the emergence of contemporary African dance). Another experiment was deliberately anti-spectacular, namely *Potlatch, dérives* (Potlatch, Excesses) involving dancers, philosophers, and simple members of the audience. Appointed director of the Centre Chorégraphique in Montpellier, Monnier developed an original training program, dubbed "e.x.e.r.c.e.," fully consonant with her choreographic ventures. Other collaborative efforts have included the Lyon Ballet Opera (*Slide*) and the Royal Swedish Ballet (*Natt 8 Rose*).

her style

Monnier is clearly wary of routine, especially the routine that can sneak up on an established artist. Her career should be discussed not in terms of cycles but of unique works that never seem to relate to one another, even though (hidden) links emerge among all of them. Indeed, it is hard to compare *Tempo 76*, in which she explored movement in unison on a surface of green grass, to *La Place du singe* (The Monkey's Place) in which she shared the stage with dynamic author Christine Angot, to *Publique*, with its rock ambience to music by P. J. Harvey, and *Gustavia*, an unexpectedly burlesque encounter between Monnier and Spanish dancer Maria La Ribot. She sometimes loses the audience, but the curious among them recognize her desire to constantly reinvent herself through choreographic encounters that generate friction (and vice versa). The slender, youthful-looking choreographer has also created many links with the rest of Europe, premiering works in Berlin and Vienna. Finally, she displays a distinct sense of humor, inserting vocalist Philippe Katerine and his album *Robots après tout* (Robots After All) into *2008 Vallée*, where she and her dancers joyfully indulged in cross-dressing and music-hall numbers—absolutely *fab*. Her next craze was the legendary ballerina Anna Pavlova, whom Monnier revived on stage—in her own sassy way, of course.

Mathilde Monnier, *Tempo 76* (2007).

"I can't imagine working without a team, without sharing ideas, without some shift within myself. That's precisely what interests me in this profession."

Mathilde Monnier, *Gustavia* (cochoreographed with Maria La Ribot, 2008).

JOSÉ MONTALVO AND DOMINIQUE HERVIEU

José Montalvo and Dominique Hervieu,
Babelle Heureuse (Happy Babelle, 2002).

their backgrounds

José Montalvo was born in Valencia, Spain, in 1954 but grew up in France where his republican family had taken refuge. Having studied architecture and the visual arts, he came to contemporary dance thanks to Jerome Andrews. Montalvo has been receptive to various styles ranging from the Dupuys to Carolyn Carlson via Merce Cunningham and Alwin Nikolais.

Dominique Hervieu, born in 1962, trained as a gymnast before moving into classical and then contemporary dance. In 1981 she met Montalvo, who began choreographing well-received solos for her. In 1988 the pair moved up a step by founding the Montalvo/Hervieu Company, providing fertile terrain for their whimsical approach to dance rich in music and imagery. From 1998 they worked out of the Centre National Chorégraphique in Creteil (outside Paris), until 2007 when they were named directors of the Théâtre National de Chaillot, which they have turned into a palatial venue for dance—of all kinds.

their style

Following the early solos devised by Montalvo for Hervieu, the team elaborated a more lasting style with works such as *Double Trouble* (1993) and *Paradis* (1997). Employing a collage technique—one of the more remarkable inventions of twentieth-century art—the duo boldly combined projected images (of giant animals, bucolic landscapes, or simply dancers filmed in the studio) with live performance. On stage, dancers from various backgrounds (classical ballet, contemporary dance, hip-hop) "responded" to the projections. Describing themselves as "contemporary baroque," Montalvo/Hervieu display great musicality ranging from Jean-Philippe Rameau (*Les Paladins* in operatic form, *On danSe* in ballet version) to Gershwin (*Porgy 8 Bess* in operatic form, *Gershwin* in ballet version). As one work followed another, Montalvo steadily became the man who conceived the imagery while Hervieu became the woman behind the dance. Given their appeal to the general (and international) public—some of their pieces were specially designed for young audiences—they have been criticized for a certain theatrical "universalism." But that would be to understate their sensitive, intelligent approach to movement. They feel that hip-hop moves are as at home in the theater as classical figures. Their upcoming project addresses the myth of Orpheus—and his doppelgängers. Once again, Montalvo/Hervieu set illusion into motion and dance with emotion.

"We're like George Gershwin in the way we shift from academic to popular, registers that can push each other along rather than ignoring each other."

José Montulvo and Dominique Hervieu, *On danSe* (We're DanCing, 2005).

JOSEF NADJ

Josef Nadj, *Les philosophes* (The Philosophers, 2001).

his background

Josef Nadj was born in 1957 in Kanjiza, a town in the former Yugoslavia just a stone's throw from the Hungarian border. At an early age he became interested in the arts, both visual and martial. Having attended the School of Fine Arts in Budapest, Hungary, he moved to France in 1980. There he became hooked on mime, going from Étienne Decroux's school to that of Marcel Marceau, followed by lessons in dance, both classical and contemporary. Having danced for the likes of Mark Tompkins, Catherine Diverrès, and François Verret, in 1986 he founded his own company, Théâtre Jel. His first work, *Canard pékinois* (Peking Duck) was both a shock and a hit—its theatricality won Nadj a notoriety far beyond his expectations. It was followed by *Sept peaux de rhinocéros* (Seven Rhinoceros Skins), *Comedia tempio*, and *Les Échelles d'Orphée* (Orpheus' Ladders), not forgetting his work with the national circus school in Châlons, *Le cri du Caméléon* (The Cry of the Chameleon). In 1995 Nadj was named director of the Centre National Chorégraphique in Orléans. His work took a new turn with *Les philosophes* (The Philosophers, 2001), which combined photography and video art with his choreographed moves. Invited to the Avignon Theater Festival in 2006, Nadj presented *Asobu* (Play) and a performance, *Paso Doble*, in conjunction with the Catalonian painter, Miquel Barceló. Once again, it was a smash.

his style

Right from *Canard pékinois* the Nadj style was clear. Heavily influenced by his roots as well as his taste for theater, circus, and the visual arts, Nadj drew inspiration from his hometown for this piece: the curtain rose on a table—for a banquet, perhaps—and characters with heavy makeup like so many ghostly celebrants seemed to come and go. It also featured Nadj's recipe of improbable creatures (men with animal heads) and props (such as suitcases and chairs) subverted from their ordinary use. Finally, there was a bodily construction through actor-dancers who fell, glided, tangled, and extricated themselves. The theatrical influences of Polish artist and director Tadeusz Kantor and German choreographer Pina Bausch are clearly present, yet Nadj cultivates his own special language through striking *tableaux vivants*, as seen in *Entracte* and *Petit psaume du matin* (Little Morning Psalm, featuring Dominique Mercy who was in fact a dancer from the Wuppertal Tanztheater). Nadj has drawn inspiration from texts by Bruno Schulz, Franz Kafka, and Raymond Roussel. His perfectly masculine style—sometimes leavened by the presence of a female soloist—is also rich with music performed live on stage by his close collaborator, Akosh Szelevényi. *Entracte* (2008) generates a new dialogue between movement and poetic moment—a woman carried by her partner uses her feet as brushes on a blank sheet. Nadj likes to say that some day he'll do something other than dance, but that seems hard to believe.

"As one work has followed another I have steadily focused my costumes on an archetype of stage dress: everyone is there in a black suit—non-specific, ready to move in any direction. I want a neutral costume open to any and every development."

Josef Nadj, *Entracte* (2008).

LLOYD NEWSON

Lloyd Newson, *The Cost of Living* (film, 2004).

his background

Born in Australia in 1957, Lloyd Newson studied psychology at the University of Melbourne prior to devoting himself to dance. He danced with the New Zealand Ballet before moving on to something else: his own work. In the 1980s he emigrated to London and studied at the London Contemporary Dance School all the while retaining a postpunk energy and enthusiasm for entertainment and political commitment. After spending a few months with the One Extra Dance Theater and the Extemporary Dance Theater, where he choreographed irreverent pieces such as *Breaking Images* and *Beauty, Art, and the Kitchen Sink,* he founded the DV8 Company with Nigel Charnock, Michelle Richecoeur, and Liz Ranken. They spearheaded a rejuvenation of the contemporary British scene. Today Newson is the sole artistic director of DV8 ("Deviate"); a keen image-maker, he also makes films and videos of dance that have garnered prizes around the world, such as *Dead Dreams of Monochrome Men* (1988) and his masterwork, *Enter Achilles* (1995), which also exist as ballets for the stage. The overtly militant homosexual Newson remains deliberately aloof yet is also—and above all—one of the most important choreographers of the past twenty years.

his style

It is clear that dance—and, to a certain extent, theater—serves Newson's activist themes. In *Enter Achilles,* the Australian Londoner recreated the atmosphere of a frankly virile pub in which homophobia is experienced as a battleground, magnified here through dance in which nobody plays the fool. In the Thatcher era, Newson waged constant combat against laws that still repressed homosexuality.

In 2005 Newson's astonishing, tightly controlled cabaret piece, *Just for Show,* featured a woman doing a striptease and a man selling his illness to the audience like a lost leader. There is always a distance here between irony and fatalism. DV8's expressive idiom is simultaneously energetic and emotional, the result of long work based on suggestions by the performers—a gesture that begins as a slap may end as a caress.

To Be Straight With You (2008), based on dozens of testimonies, flirts with tragedy somewhat more. As one work follows another—which Newson never revives, arguing that a two-year tour is sufficient—he has assembled a gallery of fascinating characters such as Miss Pussy (Diana Payne Myers, an ageing lady who gambols on stage with a young dancer) and David O'Toole, the fantastic legless dancer in *The Cost of Living.* Newson follows his own path in exemplary fashion—a long way from hype.

Lloyd Newson, *Bound to Please* (1997).

ALAIN PLATEL

Alain Platel, *vsprs* (2006).

"The finest compliment is maybe reading from time to time that the Ballets C de la B have acquired a 'style.'"

his background

Born in Belgium in 1956, Alain Platel had a first "incarnation" as an orthopedic educator before becoming a self-taught performing artist. It was in 1984 that he assembled friends and associates to found a collective in Ghent; the name he chose, Ballets C de la B, resounded like a challenge to the academicism then current in Belgium, especially following the Béjart era, which not only made a lasting mark on people but also paralyzed an entire generation of up-and-coming choreographers. The growing stature of Platel, with his dance grounded in everyday life, became apparent with *Emma* in 1988, *Bonjour Madame…* in 1993, and *La tristezza complice* in 1995. Platel also opened the Ballets C de la B to other choreographers, Sidi Larbi Cherkaoui and Koen Augustijnen having made their debuts with the company.

his style

It was not until the 1990s that Platel's reputation extended beyond his circle of admirers in Belgium. And when the Théâtre de la Bastille in Paris programmed the lengthily titled *Bonjour Madame, comment allez-vous aujourd'hui, il fait beau, il va sans doute pleuvoir, et cetera* (Morning, Madame, How Are You Today, The Weather's Nice, It Will Probably Rain, Etcetera), the enthusiasm of some early French audiences was matched by incomprehension. This theater of the body was so anchored in reality that some people spoke of "documentary dance," far from the fashionable approaches adopted by other Flemish choreographers such as Anne Teresa De Keersmaeker and Wim Vandekeybus. Platel's performers danced, of course, but were often circus performers or actors. Musicians were ubiquitous, as were opera singers, and performed between sections. Meanwhile, dancers spoke lines—tales interrupted by trances or tears. In short, the performers lived their lives. And to further underscore the realism—which sometimes had a dream-like quality—Platel recreated on stage a desolate shopping mall with packs of dogs, a bumper-car ride, and a mountain of underwear. His choreography is composed of solos that display an animal grace, improvisations that draw on hip-hop and the martial arts, and ensemble work that features brusque movements. This child of the flat country recounts a world of woes, a land that looks to God or, more reliably, to others. The live music played in *lets op Bach*, *Wolf*, *vsprs*, and *Pitié!* works to comfort these lonely hearts. Platel is open to collaboration outside his own company; in *Nightshade* he called upon a stripper, and in *Because I Sing* at the Roundhouse in London he worked with a choir. He has also made a film about the Ballets C de la B, *Out of Context*, which is also the title of a recent dance piece and which sums up this atypical character.

Alain Platel, *lets op Bach* (Something About Bach, 1998).

ANGELIN PRELJOCAJ

his background

Born near Paris in 1957 to parents who had left Albania, Angelin Preljocaj initially studied classical ballet before moving to contemporary classes with Karin Wahner at the Schola Cantorum. Among other side trips, Preljocaj took lessons with Merce Cunningham in New York, then joined the Centre National de Danse Contemporaine in Angers. There he was noticed by Dominique Bagouet, a key figure of the 1980s dance scene in France, whose company was based in Marseille. In 1984 Preljocaj decided to follow his own instincts, and he was awarded first prize at the Bagnolet dance contest for *Marché noir* (Black Market). Henceforth at the head of his own company, Preljocaj consistently surprised audiences with the diversity of his centers of interest. He has been resident since 1996 in Aix-en-Provence, where in 2006 he moved into a futurist building designed by architect Rudy Ricciotti to serve as rehearsal studio and theater. Dubbed the "Pavillon Noir" (Black Flag), the premises are perfect for this buccaneer of French dance.

Angelin Preljocaj, *Blanche Neige* (Snow White, 2008), Céline Mariè.

his style

Like other creative choreographers of the 1980s, Preljocaj sought to avoid being trapped in one specific category. His past in classical ballet as well as contemporary dance endowed "Preljo" with a quality of composition that makes him one of the few choreographers as comfortable with the Paris Opera Ballet as with the New York City Ballet, not to mention the Bolshoi and the Lyon Opera Ballet. Many companies in search of new blood have turned to him. *Le Parc* (The Park), often reprogrammed in Paris, represents the height of a style simultaneously academic and modern. Set in a formal garden, this piece includes sophisticated a pas de deux juxtaposed with a more contemporary, careering vocabulary. In *Roméo 8 Juliette* Preljocaj followed the plot but shrewdly placed it in an urban setting, perhaps a city in the former Soviet Union. Thus he won over an audience that need no longer be alarmed by an allegedly abstract dance. As far as his work with his own dancers, Preljocaj seems to have digested both the radical quality of Cunningham and the precious quality of Bagouet. In *Annonciation* this auteur-choreographer magnificently succeeded in conveying feelings and ecstasy through movement. His many collaborations with visual artists (Fabrice Hyber, Akira Kuroda, Nicole Tran Ba Vang, Enki Bilal), musicians (Air, Laurent Garnier, Karlheinz Stockhausen), and designer Jean-Paul Gaultier lend changing hues to his work. Preljocaj can attain a virtuosity evident in works such as *Helikopter, Empty Moves,* and *Eldorado*. His versions of *The Rite of Spring* and *Les Noces* (The Wedding) reflect his personal roots. Now over fifty, Preljocaj has also decided to get back on stage himself, for a solo titled *Le Funambule* (Tightrope Walker), a variation on a poetic text by Jean Genet. A challenge worthy of the princely, angelic Preljocaj.

"I love movement. I like it when one body impacts on another, the way a word impacts on another in a piece of writing. It's like a grammar of movement."

Angelin Preljocaj, *Noces* (The Wedding, 1989), Natacha Grimaud and Gaëlle Chappaz.

MEG STUART

Meg Stuart, *Forgeries, Love and Other Matters* (2004).

her background

Born in New Orleans in 1965, Meg Stuart studied dance in New York and worked for a time with the Randy Warshaw Company. She emancipated herself with *Disfigure Study* (1991), a work that toured Europe where she finally settled in 1994, opting for Brussels, a cultural capital perhaps more approachable than Paris or London. Today she divides her time between Brussels, Zurich, and Berlin. The name of her company, Damaged Goods, sums up the choreographic theme of her "dance of disaster." Ranging between collective works (*Crash Landing*), installations, and major shows, Stuart's oeuvre constantly dwells on today's world with all those bodies adrift. Above all, she brings together dancers and visual artists, and she boldly choreographs for the likes of the Berlin Ballet and the virtuoso, classically trained contemporary dancer Mikhail Baryshnikov (*Remote*, 1997). Recent ventures, in which she sometimes dances herself (*Forgeries, Love, and Other Matters*, also featuring dancer Benoît Lachambre and composer Hahn Rowe), are highly staged compositions in which she recreates commonplace or futuristic worlds. Stuart's art is often striking—and moving. It leaves no one indifferent.

her style

Eschewing the idea of a straight and narrow career, Stuart likes to misbehave. *Disfigure Study*, premiered in 1991 and revived ten years later, is a key work in her varied career, as much as a visual study of mutant bodies as a magnificently organic piece of dance designed as a tribute to the paintings of Francis Bacon. One constant feature of Stuart's work involves inward-looking individuals who seem to seek protection from the outside world. Working with visual artists such as Garry Hill and Anne Hamilton, Stuart uses lighting and imagery to create a different outlook on choreographic language.

Stuart is also known for large-scale sets: a section of building apparently gutted by an urban disaster (*Visitors Only*, 1993), or a huge wheel (*Replacement*, 2006), indeed an outsized stairway that pays tribute to American musicals (*It's Not Funny*). In each of these experiments movement must confront some external threat: it seems as though the most difficult thing to overcome is our own fear of living. *Forgeries, Love, and Other Matters*, set in a wavy green lawn, allowed its two creators to invent a life after death [life]. This highly composed—rather than danced—piece of choreographic science fiction speaks directly to the audience. When talking about herself, Stuart is talking about us.

"[In *Disfigure* Study] I did not just want to impose stories on my body but instead show those stories the body itself could tell. Stories that live in the body. And actually this is what I still do. Only now I create more situations and contexts.... But the main theme is still the same. Asking questions and formulating problems."

Meg Stuart, *It's Not Funny* (2006).

SABURO TESHIGAWARA

Saburo Teshigawara, *Glass Tooth* (2007).

his background

Born in Tokyo in 1953, Saburo Teshigawara began by taking courses in classical ballet and the visual arts. Soon he was also doing mime, movies, and photography. But desiring above all to use his body to attain "a different understanding of the world," he decided to focus on contemporary dance, although he never lost sight of his artistic and poetic leanings. From his early solos in the 1980s to the cofounding with partner Kei Miyata of the Karas ("Raven") Company in 1985, Teshigawara has sought a choreographic language based on formal exploration that willingly engages music and performance. After presenting *Kaze no Sentan* (The Tip of the Wind) at the Bagnolet Contest in 1986, Teshigawara and the Karas Company were soon dividing their time between Asia and Europe. Teshigawara was invited to choreograph works for companies such as the Frankfurt Ballet (*White Clouds Under the Heels*, Parts I and II, 1992 and 1995), and the Ballet du Grand Théâtre in Geneva (*Para Dice*, 2002). Teshigawara is constantly building bridges, for example by spearheading the S.T.E.P educational exchange between Tokyo and London.

his style

Teshigawara is clearly an explorer of virgin lands, for his dance is influenced neither by Butoh—the leading trend in Japan since the 1950s—nor by American modern dance. Fluidity and rupture are key words for this choreographer of the serene—indeed, Zen—countenance. An understanding of his style therefore has to be found in the environment surrounding his dance. Everything begins with the body, of course, which moves across the stage in waves, exploring a vocabulary that alternates between calligraphy and innate grace in a constant dialogue with changing sets, refined lighting, and impressive overall staging. In recent years the stage has alternately been covered with grass (*Green*, 2003) and countless shards of glass (*Glass Tooth*, 2007). But perhaps his finest special effect remains Teshigawara himself, as he continues to dance dazzling solos such as *Miroku*, in which a three-sided box constantly changes through lighting to frame a dance that becomes a treatise on emotions. Teshigawara claims that changes in lighting abolish the notion of "borders," generating a feeling of "timeless ecology" rather than simply framing the movement. The breathtaking results meet the audience's expectations: a fusion between a performer's approach and the beauty of his inner world. In short, all the magic of a truly live show.

"For me, dancing means playing with air."

Saburo Teshigawara, *Glass Tooth* (2007).

TRISHA BROWN ✱ *Early Works performed in the Fabre Museum, Montpellier*

APPENDIXES

WHERE to see dance?

DANCE VENUES

UNITED STATES

Joyce Theater
175 Eighth Avenue
(at the corner of 19th Street)
Manhattan, NY 10011
+1 212 691 9740
www.joyce.org

Brooklyn Academy of Music
Peter Jay Sharp Building
30 Lafayette Avenue
Brooklyn, NY 11243
+1 718 636 4100

BAM Harvey Theater
651 Fulton Street
Brooklyn, NY 11217
+1 718 636 4100
www.bam.org

BAC Baryshnikov Arts Center
450 West 37th Street
New York, NY 10018
+1 646 731 3200
www.bacnyc.org

Yerba Buena Center for the Arts
701 Mission Street
San Francisco, CA 94103-3138
+1 415 978 2700
www.ybca.org

UNITED KINGDOM

Sadler's Wells
Rosebery Avenue
London EC1R 4TN
+44 20 7863 8198
www.sadlerswells.com

The Place
17 Duke's Road
London WC1H 9PY
+44 20 7121 1000
www.theplace.org.uk

BELGIUM

**De Singel, Internationale
Kunstcampus**
Desguinlei 25
B-2018 Anvers
+32 3 248 28 28
www.desingel.be

Kaai Theater
Sainctelettesquare 19
1000 Brussels
+32 2 201 59 59
www.kaaitheater.be

FRANCE

Théâtre de la Ville
2, place du Châtelet
75004 Paris
+33 1 42 74 22 77
www.theatredelaville-paris.com

Opéra Bastille-Palais Garnier
Place de la Bastille
75012 Paris
Place de l'Opéra
75009 Paris
+33 8 92 89 90 90
www.operadeparis.fr

Théâtre National de Chaillot
1, place du Trocadéro
75116 Paris
+33 1 53 65 30 00
www.theatre-chaillot.fr

GERMANY

Radial System V
Holzmarktstrasse 33
10243 Berlin
+49 30 288 788 50
www.radialsystem.de

Bockenheimer Depot
(The Forsythe Company)
Carlo-Schmid-Platz 1
60325 Frankfurt
+49 69 21237278
www.bockenheimer-depot.de

LUXEMBOURG

Grand Théâtre du Luxembourg
1, rond-point Schuman,
+31 352 47 08 95 1
www.theatre.lu

SWEDEN

Dansen Hus
Barnhusgatan 12–13
111 24 Stockholm
+46 8 508 990 90
www.dansenhus.se

SWITZERLAND

**Arsenic
Centre d'Art Scénique Contemporain**
Rue de Genève 57
1004 Lausanne
+41 21 625 11 36
www.theatre-arsenic.ch

**ADC Genève
(Association pour la Danse
Contemporaine)**
82–84, rue des Eaux-Vives
CH–1207 Geneva
+41 22 320 06 06
www.adc-geneve.ch

DANCE COMPANIES

UNITED STATES
Merce Cunningham Dance Co.
+1 212 255 8240
www.merce.org
Alvin Ailey American Dance Theater
www.alvinailey.org
Lucinda Childs Dance
+1 212 228 2221
www.lucindachilds.com
Martha Graham Dance Company
+1 718 681 2560
www.marthagraham.org
Trisha Brown Dance Company
+1 212 977 5365
www.trishabrowncompany.org
LA Contemporary Dance Co.
www.lacontemporarydance.org

UNITED KINGDOM
Rambert Dance Company
+44 20 8630 0600
www.rambert.org.uk
New Adventures
+44 20 7713 6766
www.new-adventures.net
Akram Khan Company
+44 20 7354 4333
www.akramkhancompany.net
Hofesh Schechter Company
+44 1273 260833
www.hofesh.co.uk

BELGIUM
Rosas
+32 2 344 55 98
www.rosas.be

FRANCE
Ballet Preljocaj
+44 4 42 93 48 00
www.preljocaj.org
Philippe Découflé Company of Arts
+33 1 48 13 05 06
www.cie-dca.com

GERMANY
Tanztheater Wuppertal Pina Bausch
+49 202 563 42 53
www.pinabausch.de

SWITZERLAND
Béjart Ballet
+41 21 641 64 64
www.bejart.ch

José Montalvo and Dominique Hervieu, *Good Morning, Mr. Gershwin* (2008). Play of scale between the dance(r) in the foreground and the projected image in the background—typical of this tandem's video-choreography.

DANCE FESTIVALS

AUSTRIA
IMPULSTANZ
www.impulstanz.com

BELGIUM
KUNSTEN FESTIVAL DES ARTS
+32 2 219 07 07
www.kunstenfestivaldesarts.be

CANADA
GUELPH CONTEMPORARY DANCE
FESTIVAL
+1 519 780 2220
www.guelphcontemporarydance
festival.com
DANCING ON THE EDGE
+1 604 689 0926
www.dancingontheedge.org

FINLAND
KUOPIO DANCE FESTIVAL
+358 50 322 5220
www.kuopiodancefestival.fi

FRANCE
BIENNALE INTERNATIONALE
DE DANSE DE LYON
+33 4 72 07 41 41
www.biennale-de-lyon.org
FESTIVAL D'AVIGNON
www.festival-avignon.com

GERMANY
TANZ IM AUGUST
+49 30 259 00 427
www.tanzimaugust.de

GREECE
ATHENS FESTIVAL
+30 210 92 82 900
www.greekfestival.gr
KALAMATA DANCE FESTIVAL
+30 272 10 83 086
www.kalamatadancefestival.gr

HOLLAND
JULIDANS
www.julidans.com
HOLLAND FESTIVAL
+31 20 788 21 00
www.hollandfestival.nl

REPUBLIC OF IRELAND
DUBLIN DANCE FESTIVAL
+353 1 679 0524
www.dublindancefestival.ie

UNITED KINGDOM
DANCE UMBRELLA
+44 20 8741 4040
www.danceumbrella.co.uk
MANCHESTER INTERNATIONAL
FESTIVAL
+44 161 238 7300
www.mif.co.uk

UNITED STATES
CELEBRATE DANCE FESTIVAL
+1 619 238 1153
www.eveoke.org/cdf.htm
DANCE CAMERA WEST
+1 213 480 8633
www.dancecamerawest.org
DANCE SALAD
www.dancesalad.org
JACOB'S PILLOW
+1 413 243 0745
www.jacobspillow.org
AMERICAN DANCE FESTIVAL
+1 919 684 6402
www.americandancefestival.org

Josef Nadj, *Last Landscape* (2005, first version), *Paysage après l'orage* (Landcape after the Storm, 2006, second version). Nadj, a total artist, can dance, paint, act, and sing, enchanting audiences with his personal visions.

INDEX OF PROPER NAMES

Abramovic, Marina 183
Acogny, Germaine 114, 224
Agati, Bruno 101
Ailey, Alvin 100, 150, 166
Amagatsu, Ushio 28, 120, 144, 188, 189
Ambasch, Daniel 150, 228
André, Jean-Baptiste 170
Andrews, Jerome 23, 234
Armitage, Karole 36, 80, 100, 101, 174, 206
Armstrong, Geraldine 101
Assaf, Roy 110, 111
Attou, Kader 94, 95, 230
Augustijnen, Koen 46, 170, 181, 240
Azevedo, Paulo 94

Babilée, Jean 143
Bagouet, Dominique 88, 146, 150, 242
Balanchine, George 80, 100, 126, 165
Balestra, Ornella 218
Barbaste, Wayne 101
Baryshnikov, Mikhaïl 34, 74, 143, 148, 150, 210, 244
Batlle, Robert 100
Bausch, Pina 11, 18, 23, 27, 36, 39, 46, 50, 52, 62, 63, 66, 120, 139, 143, 148, 163, 180, 190, 191, 194, 218, 224, 236
Béjart, Maurice 11, 28, 29, 34, 42, 46, 62, 66, 114, 120, 132, 138, 144, 145, 146, 148, 150, 152, 163, 174, 176, 206, 208, 228, 240
Bel, Jérôme 11, 36, 62, 84, 132, 139, 152, 154, 192, 193, 206, 218, 224
Beltrão, Bruno 58, 94, 194, 195
Ben Mahi, Hamid 94
Bengolea, Cecilia 183
Bennetts, Kathryn 165
Bernezet, Flavien 58
Bessy, Claude 144
Bideau-Rey, Étienne 46
Bird, Bonnie 204
Blaska, Félix 23
Boivin, Dominique 44, 146, 176
Bolze, Mathurin 170
Börlin, Jean 142
Boro, Seydou 114, 232
Bory, Aurélien 107, 170
Borzik, Rolf 52, 163, 190
Bourne, Matthew 36, 126
Bouvier, Joëlle 52, 146, 192
Brabandere, Lorenzo de 218
Brown, Camille A. 100

Brown, Trisha 80, 84, 138, 139, 150, 166, 174, 175, 180, 182, 196, 197, 248
Brumachon, Claude 110
Buffard, Alain 1, 38, 39, 166, 183
Buirge, Susan 23
Butler, John 148

Calvo, Blanca 156
Capdevielle, Jonathan 47
Carasco, Manuela 216
Carlson, Carolyn 23, 34, 62, 88, 90, 150, 164, 234
Cekwana, Boyzie 114
Chaignaud, François 183
Chamblas, Dimitri 198, 199
Charmatz, Boris 136, 139, 198, 199, 218
Charnock, Nigel 238
Cherkaoui, Sidi Larbi 5, 46, 47, 66, 170, 200, 201, 222, 240
Chettur, Padmini 120, 123
Childs, Lucinda 34, 36, 88, 90, 139
Chopinot, Régine 11, 18, 20, 46, 120, 146, 152, 174, 176, 177, 198, 206
Chouinard, Marie 78, 202, 203
Clark, Michael 80, 126, 127, 226
Collod, Anne 166
Cooper, Denis 47
Coulibaly, Serge Aimé 114
Cranko, John 165, 214
Cullberg, Birgit 210
Cunningham, Merce 11, 18, 20, 22, 28, 34, 42, 52, 84, 88, 100, 104, 138, 139, 150, 162, 164, 166, 174, 176, 177, 182, 183, 192, 196, 204, 205, 206, 234, 242

Darmet, Guy 150
De Keersmaeker, Anne Teresa 8, 28, 138, 148, 167, 176, 200, 208, 209, 222, 240
Decaillot, Claude 150
Decouflé, Philippe 11, 36, 46, 52, 58, 70, 80, 104, 107, 146, 152, 154, 164, 170, 192, 206, 207
Diverrès, Catherine 144, 236
Doisneau, Véronique 62, 192
Donn, Jorge 42, 144
Droulers, Pierre 148
Duboc, Odile 174, 198
Dubois, Olivier 70, 73
Duncan, Isadora 11, 78, 138
Dunham, Katerine 100
Dupond, Patrick 74
Dupuy, Françoise and Dominique 11, 24, 27, 180, 234
Duroure, Jean-François 232

Ehnes, Barbara 55
Eiko and Koma 144
Ek, Mats 36, 150, 210, 211
Ekson, Larrio 150
Elkins, Doug 94
Endicott, Josephine Ann 66

Fabre, Jan 7, 70, 78, 80, 81, 139, 183, 212, 213
Farber, Viola 232
Fattoumi, Héla 38, 170
Feuer, Donya 210
Flamand, Frédéric 32, 42, 44
Fokine, Michel 26
Fonteyn, Margot 34
Forsythe, William 11, 36, 70, 104, 139, 160, 165, 176, 180, 182, 183, 214, 215
Fracci, Carla 150
Fuller, Loïe 46, 138

Gadès, Antonio 132
Gallotta, Jean-Claude 20, 42, 66, 88, 110, 120, 146, 150, 170
Galván, Israel 132, 133, 216, 217
Galván, José 216
Garnier, Jacques 23, 34, 150
Gat, Emanuel 74, 110, 111
Gillot, Marie-Agnes 111, 127, 144, 211
Gilteman, Claudia 164
Glover, Savion 101
Gordon, David 150, 182
Graham, Martha 11, 22, 28, 29, 42, 84, 100, 101, 139, 144, 150, 158, 162, 176, 196, 204
Gruwez, Lisbeth 78, 81
Guillem, Sylvie 34, 74, 132, 144, 222, 226

Halprin, Anna 23, 70, 80, 138, 166, 196
Hay, Deborah 150, 182
Haydée, Marcia 214
Hervieu, Dominique, and Montalvo, José 46, 58, 59, 94, 96, 152, 180, 181, 234, 235, 251
Hightower, Rosella 220
Hijikata, Tatsumi 29, 62, 120, 143, 144, 188, 198
Hoffmann, Reinhild 143, 146, 224
Hoghe, Raimund 218, 219
Horton, Lester 100
Hoyer, Dore 224
Humphrey, Doris 28, 100, 139

Ikeda, Carlotta 120, 144
Itoh, Kim 120, 144
Izeddiou, Taoufiq 114

Jamison, Judith 100
Jobin, Gilles 186, 220, 221
Jones, Bill T. 38, 100
Jooss, Kurt 27, 139, 142, 143, 190, 210, 224
Jozic, Ivana 212

Kasai, Akira 144
Kaschmann, Truda 164
Katlehong, Via 114
Khan, Akram 38, 39, 132, 200, 222, 223
King, Alonzo 126, 127
Klunchun, Pichet 132
Kossoko, Sophiatou 117

La Ribot, Maria 154, 156, 182, 220, 232, 233
Laban, Rudolf 142
Lachambre, Benoît 62, 244
Lagraa, Abou 110
Laguna, Anna 150, 210
Lamoureux, Éric 170
Lancelot, Francine 180
Larrieu, Daniel 140, 152, 153, 154, 192
Lattuada, Francesca 170
Laurier, Angela 170
Le Gac, Yann 148
Le Riche, Nicolas 34, 143, 145
Le Roy, Xavier 84, 85
Lebrun, Thomas 70
Lecavalier, Louise 52, 62, 64–65
Lefèvre, Brigitte 23, 34, 150
Leroux, Brice 85
Li, Blanca 58, 80, 82, 83, 94, 96
Libonati, Beatrice 66
Lifar, Serge 26
Linke, Susanne 36, 143, 146, 224, 225
Linyekula, Faustin 114, 117
Lock, Édouard 52, 62, 64–65, 110, 111, 139

Maalem, Heddy 114, 118–119
Malandain, Thierry 126, 128–129
Maliphant, Russell 226, 227
Maré, Rolf de 142, 174
Marin, Andrés 132
Marin, Maguy 3, 11, 19, 20, 28, 35, 36, 58, 146, 147, 148, 150, 228, 229
Markand, Anna 143
Martin-Gousset, Nasser 70, 101
Massine, Léonide 142
Maya, Mario 216
McGregor, Wayne 36, 110, 111, 165
Mercy, Dominique 62, 63, 236
Merzouki, Mourad 58, 94, 96, 170, 230, 231
Mey, Michèle-Anne de 148, 167, 208
Millepied, Benjamin 126, 127, 176
Miyata, Kei 246
Monnier, Mathilde 85, 114, 146, 156, 232, 233

Montalvo, José, and Hervieu, Dominique 46, 58, 59, 94, 96, 152, 180, 181, 234, 235, 251
Montanari, Jean-Paul 150
Montero, Vera 80
Montet, Bernardo 114, 144
Murobushi, Ko 144

Nadj, Josef 46, 170, 172, 183, 230, 236, 237, 252
Naharin, Ohad 110
Newson, Lloyd 38, 39, 156, 226, 239
Nijinska, Bronislava 27
Nijinsky, Vaslav 26, 27, 70, 139, 142, 143, 163, 216
Nikolais, Alwin 11, 58, 59, 88, 138, 154, 164, 206, 234
Noël, Kettly 114, 117
Nureyev, Rudolf 34, 74, 165
Nunn, Michael 226

Obadia, Régis 52, 146, 192
Odums, Rick 101
Ohno, Kazuo 62, 120, 144
Okach, Opyo 114
Omarsdottir, Erna 212
Orlin, Robyn 114, 117
Ouramdane, Rachid 38, 39

Pabst, Peter 52, 163, 190
Panadero, Nazareth 62
Paxton, Steve 84, 138, 139, 150, 182, 196
Perrot, Dimitri de 171
Petit, Roland 143, 174, 176
Petronio, Stephen 80
Petton, Luc 156
Philippart, Nathalie 143
Pick, Yuval 110
Pietragalla, Marie-Claude 74
Platel, Alain 2, 11, 12, 15, 38, 46, 47, 66, 80, 114, 170, 180, 181, 200, 240, 241
Pomarès, Jean 146
Ponties, Karine 104
Preljocaj, Angelin 14, 27, 36, 55, 58, 78, 138, 146, 174, 176, 192, 242, 243
Prélonge, Michèle 152
Priasso, Philippe 44

Rainer, Yvonne 38, 84, 139, 150, 166, 196
Rambert, Marie 28, 142
Ranken, Liz 238
Rayet, Jacqueline 150
Rebaud, Dominique 176
Reyes, Eugenia de los 216
Richecoeur, Michelle 238,
Rigal, Pierre 74, 75, 76, 104, 105, 107
Rizzo, Christian 139, 168, 170, 182, 183
Robbe, Hervé 148, 174
Robbins, Jerome 100, 126, 127
Rodrigues, Lia 38
Roman, Gil 29

Romero, Pedro G. 133, 216
Rouiller, Quentin 150

Sagna, Caterina p. 192
St. Denis, Ruth 28
Salamon, Eszter 84, 85
Salengro, Christophe 58, 70, 154, 206
Sanou, Salia 114, 232
Saporta, Karine 146
Schlemmer, Oskar 156
Schweizer, Michel 85
Seiler, Nicole 104
Shawn, Ted 28
Shechter, Hofesh 110
Shivalingappa, Shantala 120, 121, 188
Siegal, Richard 104
Sifnios, Duska 144
Simola, Olivier 104
Sola, Ea 120, 123
Soler, Manuel 216
Stewart, Garry 110
Stuart, Meg 52, 55, 244, 245
Szelevényi, Akosh 236

Taylor, Paul 34, 100, 166
Teshigawara, Saburo 120, 122–123, 246, 247
Thabet, Hedi 170
Tharp, Twyla 100, 101, 150
Thierrée, James 170, 172
Tompkins, Mark 146, 236
Traoré, Fatou 170
Trevitt, William 226

Umeda, Hiroaki 104, 105, 120

Van Acker, Cindy 88, 90
Van den Broeck, Hans 46
Vandekeybus, Wim 44, 46, 80, 138, 212, 240
Varona, Alexander 226
Verret, François 36, 46, 85, 146, 150, 170, 171, 236
Vienne, Gisèle 46, 47
Viera, Tais 94

Waehner, Karin 23, 27
Waltz, Sasha 81, 180
Warshaw, Randy 244
Weidman, Charles 28
Weidt, Jean 27
Wen Hui 120, 121
Wheeldon, Christopher 126, 165
Wigman, Mary 23, 27, 144, 163, 164, 180, 224
Wölfl, VA 44
Wu Zheng 23

Xaba, Nelisiwe 114, 115

Yano, Hideyuki 29

Zighera, Marie 150
Zimmermann, Martin 171

SELECTED BIBLIOGRAPHY

Anderson, Jack.
Ballet and Modern Dance:
A Concise History.
New Jersey: Princeton Book
Company, 1993.

Banes, Sally.
Terpsichore in Sneakers:
Post-Modern Dance.
Middlestown, CT: Wesleyan
University Press, 1987.

Benbow-Pfalzgraf, Taryn.
International Dictionary
of Modern Dance.
London: St. James Press, 1998.

Copeland, Roger.
Merce Cunningham:
The Modernizing of Modern Dance.
Kindle Edition, 2009.

Klein, Susan Blakeley.
Ankoku Buto: The Premodern
and Postmodern Influences
on the Dance of Utter Darkness.
Ithaca, NY: East Asia Program,
Cornell University, 1989.

Pritchard, Jane,
and Geoffrey Marsh.
Diaghilev and the Golden Age
of the Ballets Russes: 1909–1929.
London: V & A Publishing, 2010.

Reynolds, Nancy,
and Malcolm Mccormick.
No Fixed Points: Dance
in the Twentieth Century.
New Haven, CT: Yale University
Press, 2003.

Ross, Janice.
Anna Halprin: Experience as Dance.
Berkeley: University of California
Press, 2009.

Servos, Norbert,
and Gert Weigelt (photographer).
Pina Bausch. Dance Theatre.
Munich: Kieser Verlag, 2008.

Vaughan, David, Melissa Harris,
and Merce Cunningham.
Merce Cunningham: Fifty Years.
New York: Aperture, 2005.

PHOTOGRAPHIC CREDITS

All photographs by Laurent Philippe except:

© Bettmann/CORBIS, p. 26
© P.CARON/D.AUBERT/P.FORES/CORBIS SYGMA, p. 155
Marie Chouinard, p. 202
Philippe Cibille, p. 172
Mathilde Darel, p. 47 bottom right
Guy Delahaye, pp. 178–179
© Mario Del Curto, p. 171 right
Marc Domage, pp. 1, 39 top right
Jean-Louis Fernandez, pp. 23, 68–69, 163, 173,
Anna Finke, p. 159
Thomas Gray, p. 239
Arici Graziano, p. 62
Pierre Grosbois, pp. 105 top, 107
© Hulton-Deutsch Collection/CORBIS, p. 100
Alain Julien, p. 157
Isabelle Meister, p. 91
Louise Oligny, p. 78
Uri Omi, p. 39 bottom
Johan Persson, pp. 226, 227
Katrin Schoof, pp. 86–87
© Herman Sorgeloos, p. 84
Antoine Tempé, pp. 115, 116 bottom, 118–119

The author would like to thank
Fabienne Arvers,
Christine Barbaste,
Annie Bozzini,
Catherine Facerias,
Élisabeth Lebovici,
Catherine Papeguay,
Laurent Philippe,
and, for their unwavering support,
Élisabeth Couturier and Jean-Luc Morel

In memory of H. R. Noisette

Translated from the French by Deke Dusinberre
Design: François Huertas
Copyediting: Helen Woodhall
Typesetting: Thierry Renard
Proofreading: Chrisoula Petridis
Color Separation: Reproscan, Bergamo
Printed in Italy by Graphart

Originally published in French as *Danse contemporaine: mode d'emploi*
© Flammarion, S.A., Paris, 2010

English-language edition
© Flammarion, S.A., Paris, 2011